praise for **White Men My Age**

Bonifer is an amazing poet and storyteller, who has lived a Forrest-Gumpian life, having been present for every major event in human history with a first hand account of what really happened. He has, in all of his poetry, this amazing ability to see, hear and write the events that really mattered, and capture the full attention of anyone who will listen or read. He is one of the best Occasion poets I have ever heard, keenly capturing what we all should hold onto in the moments when we honor our local and national heroes. A poet is someone who sees what others miss; someone who can pluck out and goldplate the special details happening in this grand and glorious life. This book is a chapter-based time capsule waiting to be opened and explored for all of its treasures.

> **Hiram Sims**, founder, The Sims Library of Poetry and the Community Literature Initiative; co-founder, World Stage Press; City of Los Angeles Public Library Commissioner

White Men My Age pulls you into a certain kind of blues from the other side of the tracks. Vivid poetic memories that stretch from JFK to Tiger Woods. There is an alchemy in the way Bonifer's pen cuts the paper and how the truth bleeds out and develops on the parchments. His technique is meticulous and deliberate and if you listen closely, you may hear a few swan songs.

> **Tommy Domino**, author of *Switches, Hot Wheel Tracks and Extension Cords*

Mike Bonifer has written a book of delightful, entertaining, insightful and constantly surprising poems. For more than 40 years, I've followed his path from top Disney motion picture publicist ("Tron," "Dick Tracy"), to screenwriter, producer, author, motivational speaker, innovator in using improvisation in the workplace, and other endeavors. I'm so impressed with his passion for poetry and his dedication to expressing himself with imagination and courage in this unique art form. I think you will be too.

> **Howard Green**, Senior Disney Animation Publicity Executive/Historian

Thoughtful and clever with just the right mix of experiences that apply to our modern world and society. A touch of humor here and there reminds us not to take ourselves too seriously. They type of quality writing I have come to expect from Mike Bonifer.

> **Jeff Roberts, Ph.D.**

White Men My Age is a necessary collection—surrendered from the soul and gifted to nourish the soil and landscape of poetry. Bonifer's carefully-crafted pages are soaked with poignant authenticity and catharsis stitched into every piece. In this body of work, with the unearthing of each poem, we find ourselves unraveling a crucial voice that becomes a friend. Bonifer's voice becomes a familiar echo in a hallway of truth-seekers and eager spectators as he splatters images and words onto each page like an inkblot projection of personality onto papyrus.

Ravina Wadhwani, author of *Yellow*

White Men My Age is an imperative look into the character and an assessment of one of the most reproachful, compassionate, hated, beloved, overachieving and misunderstood creatures of the known universe: the White Man in American Society in the 21st Century, as seen through the eyes of one of America's most poignant White citizens, the poet Mike Bonifer. Bonifer's brilliantly distinct poetic documentation and explication of the self navigates the reader beyond ethnicity and culture and ventures past the physical and into the spiritual realm through waves of uncertainty to arrive at the uncharted shores of enlightenment.

Carlos Ornelas, author of *Ketchup: Sopa de Gato*; Acquisitions Editor, Community Literature Initiative

BONAFIDE or "BONIFIED"—it means to make something good. It only takes one word to describe the work of *White Men My Age*…applause, APPLAUSE!

V. Kali, author of *Hymn*; Facilitator, Anansi Writers Workshop

In this collection of poems, Mike Bonifer uses a magic wand and brings us into his world. These poems will make you feel like you have a front seat at the table while he weaves each story. He is transparent, witty and poetic. You will fall in love with Rosie as he describes her entering this world in a storm. You will feel like you know his childhood friends as he lists their nicknames. *White Men My Age* is a book you will want to read over and over.

Jaha Zainabu, Artist-In-Residence, WomanPreach! Inc.; author of *I Am Writing to Tell You* and *365:2013 A Poem a Day Series*

Clever, creative writing! I have known Mike nearly all my life. I can feel the emotion that he evokes by describing his life experiences. "Regret" is particularly touching. He has delivered a gift for us to enjoy!

Jerry Wehr, M.D., grade school classmate

The poems are truly moving. I am looking forward to reading them many, many times. My hat is off not only to Mike's intellect, but the motivation and discipline it must take to create artwork at this level. BRAVO!

Marty Newman, high school classmate

Bonifer looks back on life and observes relationships with clear eyed memory and empathy—the hard love of and for a father, the birth of a grandchild, of goats and GOATS, of witting pretenders who mock and are unwittingly mocked by fate. His poetry is accessible and erudite without pretension, expressive of catholic truths with a cadence that draws and locks in the reader who is free to feel as well as understand.

Bill Powers, college classmate

white men my age

white men my age
poetry by Mike Bonifer

World Stage Press
Verse from the Village

World Stage Press
Verse from the Village

White Men My Age
© 2025 Mike Bonifer
ISBN: 978-1-952952-75-3

First Edition, 2025

All rights reserved. No part of this publication may be reproduced, distributed, or transmitted in any form or by any means, including photocopying, recording, or other electronic or mechanical methods, without the prior written permission of the publisher, except in the case of brief quotations embodied in critical reviews and certain other noncommercial uses permitted by copyright law.

Printed in the United States of America

Edited by Rachel Cartwright
Cover Design by Mike Bonifer and Emily Anne Evans
Layout Design by Haidyn Reynolds

This book is dedicated to the poets of the Anansi
Writers Workshop and its director V. Kali. You
have blessed the poetry printed here, as you do all
the work brought to your stage, with the wisdom
of the ancestors, the fire of the sun and the soul
of the moon. Every time I walk out your door the
world is a little better than when I walked in.
And so we go....

Poems

Preface xv

Pick up a pen inked with your memories

Lean Methodology 5
Give Time 7
small democracies 9
Prayer for the Empty-Handed 10
Remote 11
No Cereal Blues 13
Faith in Industry 15
Hiram Sims Sends His Regrets 17
Water Witch 18
White Men My Age 20

I shoot hoops in all seasons...

Wilt 27
Scapegoat 31
Braden at the Plate 34
Abebe Bikila 36
Ode to the Ireland Spuds 39
Tiger Pa 42

Eyes of the band boys widen

The Road Is Our Religion 49
Basement House Groove 51
A Story About Maury 53
Nineteen 56
No Prestige 57
Escape Room 59
Hazer 62
This is Not an Endorsement 64
Complicity 67
King of the Student Body 68

You have the eyes of the ancients

Rosie Is Here 75
Biographies of the Saints 77
Maria of Bristol Farms 81
Blewfoot 86

How You See 88
Cello 90
Recap 91
A Chitty Chitty Bang Bang Wedding Toast
for Emily & Jeffrey 93
Jaha Tells You 95
A Thing I Know 97
Voice Mail to Bill Murray's 800 Number 98

You had that smile

Elegy For Uncle Joe 105
Last Night In The Buckaroo Bar & Grill 111
Eddie's Carolina 114
War Comes Home 116
Bad Goodbye 118
Last Words 121
Nine Lives 123
Shoes on Power Lines 124
Remains of the Bells 127
Versions of Us 129
Regret 131
V-72 133
Peripheral Vision 136
Amen Asé Aho 138

Acknowledgements 141
About the Author 143

Preface

When I began listening to and writing poetry in earnest, in 2015, at the Anansi Writers Workshop in Los Angeles, I was usually the only white man my age in attendance. As I returned week after week to witness the profoundly beautiful language that flowed from its stage, I couldn't help noticing that white men are often the villains in the stories the poets and griots share there. It took me a while to realize they are not referring to me. And a while longer to realize that they are. And even longer to realize that they are and they aren't. We are all complicit in the creation of the world we live in and the stories we share about it. Whether we want to be or not. Whether we are aware of how our history intersects with others or not. As it turns out, my complicity in the stories and poetry birthed on the Anansi Workshop's stage, through the Community Literature Initiative, and at The Sims Library of Poetry in Los Angeles, has been one of the greatest gifts that has ever come my way. Here, my complicity found its "want to be." Here, my complicity gained its awareness of our co-created histories.

White Men My Age is my life in verse. Rooted in America's heartland, where I was born and raised, flavored by relentless love for family and friends, and seasoned by many years and adventures around the world, the poetry cooks up responses to the questions: Who am I? Who are we? And the one that eventually lands on everyone's plate: Who are we to one another?

Mike Bonifer

white men my age

Pick up a pen inked with your memories

Lean Methodology

at first...
I leaned in
The Queen said
Thank you for your head
And left the rest of me for dead

I leaned in
The Water said
Together we're perfection
Then drowned me in my reflection.

I leaned in
The Wind said
Destiny turns on a word
Are you a boat? Or are you a bird?

I leaned in
The Tree said
Pay attention to the Wind
To survive you've got to bend.

I leaned in
The Stone said
If that's your game
You're going to damage your brain.

I leaned in
The Fire said
Let's not get too close
Or one of us will get burned.

I leaned in
The Turtle withdrew
Didn't say a thing
But I swear I heard it laughing.
and then...
Comes a day,
I don't know why,
I choose to lean a different way. Out for a change. Wow!
The world looks different now.

I lean over—love the view
Lean back—cool
Lean around—profound
Lean East, West, North South, Lean up, lean down.
Even a time or two
I lean all the way through.
Until it comes to me
Like a clue to Nancy Drew
We are where we lean.
Damn!
So let us lean
In all directions
Like we pray
Like we dream
Like we dance
In all all directions
Like gamblers covering bets
Like flowers finding sun
Like Forrest Gump on the run
Not every push comes to shove
Not all that's smooth is criminal
Not all the writing's on the wall
The only guarantee
That comes with a one-way lean
Is that eventually

Eventually

We fall.

Give Time
For the Sims Library of Poetry 2nd Anniversary · 15 July 2023

Please allow me to opine—
Everything beautiful begins
With the giving of time

Give time to a seed and
It will find the spring that
Carries its promise to the sun

Give time to a night sky and
It will exclaim your most
Faraway dreams with a shooting star

Give time to a child and just like that
It's a better day and
Even tomorrow might turn out okay

Give Time to Morris Day and
A dance will ensue until the clean-up crew
Has mopped up the mess you made at the party

Give time to music and
It will stop a clock and carve it
Into slices of recollected love

Give time to love and
Whenever you reach a fork in your path
It will whisper, "This is the way"

Give time to a basketball and
It will donate to the sensitivity in your fingertips,
Your focus, your timing, your flow
So that when a lover moans in the midst of your ecstatic thrall
You will say to yourself, "Thank you, basketball"

Give time to the alley behind your house and
The pup someone abandoned there
Will find a home and
The taggers will leave you alone because
When they come back to brag on their graffiti to their homies
It will be gone

Give time to Hiram Sims and
He will unpack a suitcase full of books into
A story that begins, "Remember when
There wasn't enough for the crowd to eat until
A kid stepped up with some fish and a couple loaves of bread?"

Give time to poets and
They will spit prophetic visions of
Turning their heartbreak into happiness until
Their joy becomes your own

Give time to poets and
They will describe what you would not otherwise see
With your own eyes in a hundred lifetimes

Give time to poets and
They will bleed and blend onto pages
The only words you will will ever need and
Come to heed
As truth

Give time and know that
Something beautiful is on its way
To you

small democracies

Wikipedia lists twenty-nine types of Democracies
I spell mine with a small 'd'
dêmos, common people
krâtos, force, might
force and might of common people
local, ethical, and concrete
practical and pedagogical.
a mode of associated living
participatory association
a conjoint communicated experience
non-linear decision-making
kairotic timekeeping
the flow state of a group mind

favor the many instead of the few
perceive the full import of one's activity
appraise your relationship to the environment
actions of others give point and direction to your own
break down barriers of class, race, and national territory
voluntarily unite around an everyday concern
concern yourself with public safety

the planting of trees
the installation of a stop sign
the paving of speed bumps
the shutting down of toxic wells
the making of public art

discourse of citizen educators
education in self-governance
beneath politics and policy
beyond do-goodery
sums are greater than the addition of their parts
outcomes are more potent than goals attained

Prayer for the Empty-Handed

Lay down your gun
Weave a basket with reeds of belonging
Fill it with music
Feed the song-less multitudes

Lay down your gun
Pick up a pen inked with your memories
Stain a page with your pain
Make a paper airplane and let it fly

Lay down your gun

Release your notions that it is a thermometer measuring the heat of your anger— A gauge indicating the pressure imposed by your imagination— A commercially-bred GMO penis substitute double-helixing dominance and love— A companion cast in
        the hollow of your loneliness—
     A microphone languaging
   your darkest thoughts—
 A needle that draws
the blood you drink
as your god—

Lay down your gun
Center your sight on a silhouette
dancing into the illumination of a dawning day
Realize it is you

Lay down your gun
Let your trigger finger be
the first limb of a tree
a child's hand will grasp
to begin the climb of a lifetime

Lay down your gun
Lay down your gun
Lay down your gun

Remote

Who controls you controls the world

In the hands of a child
The view is as new as my wobbly walk
My world seen in animated shards
In the squash and stretch of characters
Who bounce manically through
Neoned cities and cartooned yards

In your dance with adolescence
You crash the party with me
Quest for exceptions to the rules
Push permissions to their limits
Mine screens for naughty nuggets
I can flash tomorrow at school

When a teen gets hold of you
You dimensionalize the secrets
We exchange on phones all day
You are the beacon zeroing in
On a mirrored world where
Everyone looks and acts like me

The stakes get higher when you land
In the hands of a romancer
What kinds of choices do they make?
Are they restless, uncertain, contentious?
A promiscuous changer of channels?
Or respectful of my program tastes?

In the paws of a brother-in-law
You are a weapon that holds us hostage
We are Stockholmed into rooting
For his alma mater in a game
Our freedom is a pinhole in a camera
That sees the world as a wrestling ring

In middle ages you are a wizard's wand
That prestos us from contented to alarmed
One minute we are dozing after dinner
To re-runs of *Fresh Prince* or *Friends*
The next we are awakened by news
That a loser has declared himself a winner

As I lay here in a hospital bed
Surrounded by screens that maintain
The vital signs in a failing system
The control I need from you
Is to shut them all down
Turn off the wider world
Leave me here with memories
Of who and what I love
And why
Make me remoteless
The world immediate
Touchable
Kissable
Real
With no screens
Or secrets
Or questions
Or choices
Between me
And the last faces I see

No Cereal Blues
Inspired by an improvised song by
Lyric Lewis and The Groundlings · October 2022

You know how it is in the mornin'
Gotta get that engine started
Go to pour a bowl and—*oh no!*
We're outta cereal!

Nothin on top of the fridge
Where Count Chocula normally is
How'm I gonna make it to lunch
With no morning love from Cap'n Crunch?

No Lucky Charms, no Frosted Flakes
No Kix or Special K
I don't find my Apple Jacks
It'll ruin my whole day

No cereal!
No cereal!
A cereal killer has struck
I'm all outta luck
Lost and down low
No Wheaties in my bowl
Hear the silence of the spoons
I got the No Cereal Blues
Yes I do
Yes I do

We're out of Chex and Cheerios
Can't find my Honeycomb
With a kitchen missing Golden Grahams
Can't call this house a home

Don't bother breaking me an egg
Oatmeal? Ha-ha, stop
I need what I eat in the mornin'
To Snap and Crackle and Pop

Daddy left his Grape Nuts
Mama her Müeslix
We fed it all to the parrot
And now we're in a fix

No cereal!
No cereal!
A cereal killer has struck
We're all outta luck
Lost and down low
No Boo Berry in my bowl
Hear the silence of the spoons
I got the No Cereal Blues
Yes I do
Yes I do
So do you
So do you
What are we gonna do…

For breakfast?

Faith in Industry
An homage to Clark Ashton

The Artist hoists an old steamfitter's
monkey wrench as long as a baseball bat
over a terrycloth bathrobed shoulder
In unlaced work boots shuffles
his achy morning body
down a gravelly asphalt drive
toward a highway constipated
with metal animals stampeding
slow-motion in two directions
to their respective watering holes

Beneath the burden of his wrench
he treads slowly in his robe
back and forth along the road
the heaviness of his tool
weighing on his weary soul
Raises his roadside hand
blessing the motoring congregation
with a one-word prayer—
Faith!

Dropping his wrench he
climbs a Tower he has made
from the remains of a fire escape
Cranks a metal wheel repurposed
from an abandoned Bessemer mill
to send a grappling hook
left in the ashes of an industrial fire
to the end of a thirty-foot crane
rescued from a train yard
out over a border fence made of
oxidized steel eel men he has welded
and chained to dancing metal sperms

Cranks the hook out to where
the traffic waits and and back
salvaging souls of commuters

Reels them back over the
eel-and-sperm-guarded border
to the friendly homespace
on his side of the divide

When he has saved
a sufficient number of souls
he climbs down from his Tower
and turns a decommissioned tugboat wheel
that spins a retired sawmill blade
atop a mast made of windmill parts
he won with a twenty-dollar bid
at a farm foreclosure auction
This opens a hole to heaven
where commuters can be at peace

With twin jackhammer blades
orphaned at a construction site
scissoring atop a spire built
with demolition site rebar
he animates with a foot pedal
liberated from a broken pottery wheel
he closes the hole to heaven
by stitching up the sky

Climbs back up his Tower and
unfurls the morning paper to
catch up on what happened
beyond the reach of his rescue crane
beyond the penetrations of metal sperms
and the ken of rusty steel eel men
Every now and then a car horn
honks a greeting from a commuter
whose soul he saved on another day
He looks up from the news
Raises a scepter he sculpted from
the dipstick of a dead Chevrolet
and hails the grateful commuter
Faith!

Hiram Sims Sends His Regrets

At five-twenty-five PM on the day before an event
At which he is scheduled to present
I receive a text from Mister Hiram Sims:
I got sick yesterday and my voice is entirely gone.
I have strep throat. I'm hoping rest will help me.

It comes as no surprise whatsoever
that a co-founder of the World Stage Press
which publishes at least a book of poetry a month
and has released over a hundred volumes to date…

Who runs the Community Literature Initiative
which gives skills and voices and stages to
thoughtful and creative folks with something to say
who need places to write and say it…

Who turned a suitcase into a library
Then his garage into a library
Then a pre-school into a library
Open to the public and private poets of his city…

Who is working with his wife and father
(now that he and Charisse got their garage back)
to remodel their home to make more room for
their one son and five daughters…

Who is a regular on the poetry scene in L.A.
and a growing presence across the nation…
It comes as *no surprise at all*
that the man's voice needs a vacation.

What comes as a surprise…
What *always* comes as a surprise
is the poetry that flows from Hiram Sims
even when the voice is not his.

Water Witch

One

My grandma can find water underground
With the forked limb of a peach tree.
Me? I divine by a more pedestrian method—
I ask around.
I ask her one day when I'm eight—
She and I are feeding trash to a fire
In a rusty red barrel
Back behind her house—

How do you find water the way you do?
She smiles at me with spark-lit eyes,
I'm a witch, didn't you know that?
The barreled flame soars
Devouring yesterday's news.
I mean a water witch,
It's what people call a person like me
Who can find an underground spring
With the branch of a tree.
They call it witching for water.
Or dowsing.
Or divining.
I hear not a word of her explanation.
My eight-year-old head
Has been hijacked by a revelation--
My grandmother is a witch!
It explains so much.
Why her hydrangeas grow abnormally large,
And an ear of her corn is the size of my arm,
How a voice that can carry a church choir
So far off-key it won't find its way back
'Til the following Sunday
Can cackle conversantly with chickens,
And bring cats to her back door
That none of us has seen before.
My story carries me away
Like like firebats
From a burning cave—
My grandmother is a witch!

Two

Grandmother witches for water
In order that we might make a lake
On our family's farm
Fed by a spring she locates
Blades of grass speak to her
In a hundred windy tongues
As she walks a field,
Peachtree fork in fingertips
Branch in breeze
Imagines she's balancing the earth
On the soles of her feet,
Letting its water flow into her
And tell her its secrets.
Crosses a spot
Where her body shivers
The fork quivers,
Grass quiets so water can speak.
Here. Look here.

Three

My grandmother the witch
Abandons Earth on Christmas Day
A reminder to her church and its choir
That a diviner can unlock heaven
In her own time
With a key of her own design
Make her own holiday
When the occasion of her leaving us
Weaves memories of her departure
Into the arrival of baby Jesus

White Men My Age

One

When we hear over the intercom
in our fifth-grade classroom
that JFK has died in Dallas
class clown William
clutches his heart
falls to the floor
groans "They got me!"
like a fallen movie villain

White men my age
grew up experiencing
death at a distance
And clowning any
pain that's not our own

Two

Men the same age as mine
waited for seventeen years
after he died to say
their pastor molested them
when they were boys
Got his name blasted
at last off limestone
monuments to his bloated
parade-floated public facade

Confusing religion with faith
is the biggest mistake
white men my age make
The second biggest is
leaving justice up to God

Three

We nickname all our friends—
Kunk, Feets, Cuss, Beetle,
Vondy, Beaver, Heg, Weasel,
Possum, Gopher, Schmuck, Snip
Colonel, Dip, K.O., Chip
Bagoo, Bitchin, Bonny, Ghost
Gibby, Gummy, Goldie, Toast

I do appreciate this
particular feature
of white men my age—
Our lifelong identities
as comic book entities

Four

Revel in firing employees
Stress about the second home
Moan over the cost of a boat
Complain about the help
Credit work she did to yourself
Pose as a self-made man
when your climb began
with help from daddy's hand
Have a calculator in your head
that computes the difference between
paying a contractor what they're due
and what it will cost them to sue
What you have will never be enough
Your consolation comes with knowing
who in the world has less than you
And who has to pay through the nose
for what you inhale for free

Two wrongs may not make a right
Those same two wrongs rewarded
are my guarantee that you're white
and the same generation as I

Five

Doctor Greg built a hospice
to care for the dying poor
Big Al the paramedic died
saving a woman from a fire
Jay and his wife outfit classrooms
and baseballers in the DR
These men are among the most
beautiful humans I've met
And yet and yet and yet
before I conveniently forget—
That white man my age
who called you by the
wrong name in a meeting
because he was blinded
by your melanin?

That was me

I shoot hoops in all seasons...

Wilt

Had my first ten-foot hoop
Bright orange ring and white nylon net
Mounted on carpentered backboard
Bolted to a hickory pole
On the family farm back in Indiana
Where basketball was religion
Where congregations gathered
On Friday and Saturday nights
To worship in glowing churches
Young gods in holy wars
Of zone and man-to-man
Fast break and pattern ball

Local legends fill these halls
Pete Gill, Jumpin' Jack Steinhart
Junior Gee, Larry and Bugsy Humes, Dave Small
Oscar, The Van Arsdales, Rick Mount
I am them all
Pass me the ball

I shoot hoops in all seasons
When the net is frozen
And my bounce-less Voit will not drop through
When the grass has given up
And my court is muddy
And covered by cardboard in spring
Baked hard with tractor tracks in summer
That I wear away by fall
Me and that basket and that ball
Morning, noon, night by yard light
Put the ball in the hoop
Shoot. Shoot. Shoot.

Never mind getting animals fed
Or homework done
Never mind getting ready for church
Or coming to supper when Mother calls

Put the ball in the hoop
Follow through like Coach taught me to
Shoot. Shoot. Shoot.

With each shot I move another step
Closer to the pantheon
Of gods who fly ball to basket
On Friday and Saturday nights
While people scream their names
And reverence their game with passion
They don't give to Jesus Christ

Who I most want to be is Wilt Chamberlain
Of the Philadelphia Seventy-Sixers
Later the Warriors and Lakers
Wilt the Stilt, The Big Dipper
Who plays his games on Sunday
Like the major gods do
The object of my mania
Once scored a hundred points
Against the New York Knicks
In a game played in Hershey, Pennsylvania

A hundred points! These high school boys
These Wildcats, Spuds and Yellowjackets
Do well to go for eighteen or twenty
Wilt went for a hundy,
That's me. Who I want to be
Thirteen. That's our number
Me and Wilt say fuck your luck
We'll make our own
I wear a rubber band on my left wrist like Wilt does
To call attention to the fact
That Wilt and me are not our jewelry
One day I'll wear knee pads below my knees like Wilt
To call attention to the fact
That your puny ass will never
Live up to my majesty
Shoot. Shoot. Shoot.

Shoot like Wilt shot the ball that night in Hershey
When he, a historically pathetic shooter of the freebie—
Because Wilt does not take charity—
Sinks twenty-eight of thirty-two from the stripe
Proving that when Wilt and me put our minds to it
Ain't nothin' we can't do
Bank the ball through the hoop
Shoot. Shoot. Shoot.

For a player as big and powerful as I
I am remarkably humble
Help old ladies into hotel elevators
My tips put smiles on the faces of waiters
With grown-ups I'm aloof
With children kind
I drink half a gallon of milk at halftime,
My fall-away shot cannot be blocked
I may go for a hundred and twenty this time
Watch me put the ball in the hoop
Scream my name
Shoot. Shoot. Shoot.

Comes a day I realize that my chances of being
Seven-foot-one and spending a year
With the Globetrotters like Wilt are nil
The only way I'll dunk like the Dipper
Is by standing on the steps of a ladder
That is not Wilt Chamberrlain's dad
Calling from the barn right now
To come and water the cows
I cannot even jump and touch the rim
But that doesn't stop me
From wanting to be him
Wanting Hef and Quincy and Miles
As my L.A. pals
Building a house in the Hollywood Hills
With no right angles
In its architecture
Decorated with oversized furniture,

And mind you, before my story's through
I fully intend
To bed ten thousand women
Like Wilt would do

Shoot.
Shoot.
Shoot
Put the ball in the hoop
Make my own luck
Score a hundred
Be Wilt Chamberlain

Scapegoat

Best Night of My Life.
We were ahead in top of the eighth
One out, one runner on base
When Castillo fouled a pitch
High into the night sky
Oh baby, here it came
A comet sent by the baseball gods
Stamped with my name

How can I not reach out to accept
A gift from the baseball gods?
I mean, what are the odds?
One in five hundred sixty-six
When you're in my seat
Aisle Four, Row Eight, Seat One Thirteen
I'm an accountant by trade
I know these things

I touched but did not catch the gift
Diverted its flight away from Moises' mitt
Now Moises is pissed!
Taking his cue, everyone is booing me
For doing what they would've done if they were me
After that, our heroes fell that night
And I had to go into hiding
Worst Night of My Life.

I am the reason, according to the media
That a magic season presto'd tragically
I am the goat who cursed a city
Destroyer of a generation
Of "I was there" stories
Told by one thousand two hundred times
The number of people
Who were actually there
I know the numbers
I'm an accountant, goddammit
A motherfuckin' CPA!

Why you lookin' at me like that?
And dumping beer on my head?
Why am I the villain in this story?
I didn't boot the ground ball at short
Later in the inning
I didn't lose the game, bitch
Wasn't on the mound giving up hits
Why you making me
A receptacle for your misery?

I am not the reason
You didn't pass the bar exam
Not the reason you got that DUI
Or that your kid got sick
Or your dog ran away
Or your faucet's running dirty water
I am not the high school teacher
Who made a pass at your daughter

You don't know this about me,
I'm really good with numbers
At measuring the difference
Between what's on the books
And what's in the bank
I count, I keep track
I know exactly what you owe me—
An apology

You turned my name into the butt
Of seven thousand two hundred twenty-two jokes
That spread like an oil spill
On a stagnant river already polluted
By your life's regrets
Your plasticized illusions
Your drowned sorrows
And the wreckage of your sunken dreams

I know the numbers
I'm an accountant, goddammit
A motherfuckin' CPA!
I know the difference between
What you do and what you say
What I did is what you would've done
When I made the mistake
Of believing a ball was a gift of grace
And not the fall I was about to take

My bad. I admitted it
But my bad wasn't even a millionth
Of what you came at me with
I know the numbers
An apology is owed
That's the principal
The interest is your atonement

How about you make us whole again
By healing wounds you inflict on a daily basis
With the fuckwaddery of your ways
Like the world stole your ticket
To a lottery you weren't going to win anyway
I know the odds, I totalize for a living
In percentages I see fate—
To get a break, you give a break

I know the numbers
I'm an accountant, goddammit
A motherfuckin' CPA!
An apology is owed
And you can count on this
There will be a day
When one way or another
You. Will. Pay.

Braden at the Plate
For Bill Powers, who is generous to six-year old baserunners

An industry softball game
Played by Self-Important Players
Happens every Wednesday at six
At a ball field in the shadows
Of Twentieth Century Fox
Sons of Men You've Heard Of
Aggressive bros with prestige diplomas
And ancestries engraved in gold
Get their egos on in
Edgy competitions

The batboy in these games is Braden
An after-thought of six
In pee-wee cleats
Son of a Senator's son
Who's a rising star at Morris
By the way he takes swings
With the bats he fetches
And runs down foul balls
You can tell Braden aches
To get in the game
He dreams of the day
He'll be old enough and big enough
To step to the plate like his dad
And the wisecracking swingers
Who play in the Important Game
"I'll play," he'll say
When a team lacks a player
When the players ignore his offer
He wants it even more
He'll show them one day for sure
Every game holds inherent
The possibility of a miracle
Braden gets his one Wednesday
In the final inning of an outing
That is otherwise uneventful
"Grab a bat, son," says his dad
Who'd agented a deal
For Little Man to get his turn

To step to the plate with an
Aluminum Eaton he can barely swing
Braden does what he dreams
With a mighty lurch at the lofted ball
A second miracle! He connects!
Bumps a spinning roller
Down the third-base line
"Run!" shouts his dad.
"Go!" screams his team.
Braden races toward first base
As if chased by howling dogs
A hard charging third baseman
A Paramount exec by day
Bare-hands the ball on the run
Slings it to first while falling
A tick ahead of the hustling boy
"Out!" crows the thrower
"Safe!" exclaims his dad
Their beef ignites the debate
That animates their lives—
Who is wrong? Who is right?
Both teams rage over
The status of the runner
Who stands on first in tears
Mortified by the mess he caused
And his dad in the middle of it all
Losing the fight for leniency
The boy is ruled out at first and
Sent apologetically to the bench

On their drive home that evening
Braden unlaces his cleats
Throws them in the backseat
Vows to himself he'll never play
His father's stupid game again
Turns his dreams to the sticker
A skull with emerald eyes
He'll add to his skateboard
While he learns to do an olly

Abebe Bikila

Abebe Bikila
Ethiopia's favorite son
Won the '60 Olympics Marathon gold
Running barefoot through the streets of Rome
Set a new world record in bare feet
Repeated the feat in shoes
In '64 in Tokyo
First marathoner to go gold
Twice in a row

Flipped his Beetle
On an Addis Ababa highway in '69
First a paraplegic
Then a wheelchair athlete
In table tennis and archery
Died in '73
Cerebral hemorrhage, done
Age of forty-one

Abebe Bikila
Ethiopia's favorite son
Say his name in a restaurant
In Little Ethiopia
Waitress'll smile at you and
Bring you extra sambu—

Wait a second—
Run it back
Begin again
Abebe Bikila won
The 1960 Olympics Marathon
Barefoot!
Ran twenty-six miles, three hundred eighty-five yards
Barefoot!
Forty-two point one nine five kilometers
Barefoot!

Chased by sixty men in shoes, he ran
Barefoot!
Had shoes, they gave him blisters
So he tossed them in the trash and ran
Barefoot!
Through the crooked cobblestoned hills of Rome
Barefoot!
Lit by torches along the Appian Way
Barefoot!
Finished at night under the Arch of Constantine
Barefoot!
In the shadow of the Coliseum
Barefoot!
Two hours, fifteen minutes, sixteen seconds
Barefoot!
Set the world record
Barefoot!
Took the gold
Barefoot!
Broke the tape and kept running on his tiptoes
Barefoot!
Said he could run another 10K easy
Barefoot!
Ran himself into history
Barefoot!

After that—
Abebe needs a new pair of shoes
Puma walks into the room
With cash socked away in the shoes
He will wear to win in Tokyo
That is the pinnacle, the peak
In five years he'll flip the Beetle
And lose the lease on his rented feet
In four more he'll go to his glory
That's the straight-ahead story

In the story that doesn't run straight ahead
Abebe Bikila is not dead
After breaking the tape in Rome
While still on tiptoes
It is not in place, but into the torchlight
Of a million imaginations that he runs
Is running still
In the Hills of Rome
Along Addis Ababa roads
In the restaurants of Little Ethiopia
And in this poem
Ethiopia's favorite son
Barefoot as the day he was born
Abebe Bikila

Ode to the Ireland Spuds
With love and appreciation for the 1963 Ireland Spuds high school basketball team on the 60th anniversary of our memorable year

Any year that ends in '3'
carries back me to '63
when the Ireland Spuds
made their run to the Sweet 16

No one who lived here then
will ever catch a mention
of Larry Bird's high school team
without thinking "Ireland 20, Springs Valley 19"

My teacher that season was Henrietta Allen
whose husband, Roy, was Assistant Coach
leading me to believe any big man an imposter
who does not have a Henrietta on his roster

My third-grade crush was Pamela Schitter
whose brother, Pat, made the Regional buzzer-beater
For these six decades I could never love another
who did not have such a hero for a brother

I can never watch the movie *Hoosiers*
without believing our version was better
Jimmy Chitwood didn't ride my school bus
like Dave Small and Arnie Renner

Hickory didn't hang a banner
across the highway on consecutive Saturdays
where they drank beer provided by
Stan Leinenbach's uncle after their victories

Hickory's coach did not drop his pants
to make good on a crazy promise
like our Coach Pete Gill did
in front of the local populace

Hipsters in black Chuck Taylors
might make big city fashion sense
But they'll never be as cool
as Doug Padgett or Joe Lents

Before Bill Walton UCLA'd
or Secretariat was thoroughly bred
Denny Keusch of the Ireland Spuds
set the standard for studs whose hair was red

Of men with muscular reps
dudes you're supposed to fear
I always imagine Stan and Ronny Klem
saying, Please—hold our beer

In any victory celebration
through blizzards of confetti
I can still see the smiling face
of my cousin Bill Linette

When bouncers clear a late night bar
or lawyers file a claim
I recall the firm of Eck & Voelkel
clearing out the lane

Wherever books are balanced
and the busses run on time
I give all the original credit
to Junie Wigand and Ronny Heim

A leader who's successful
wherever he or she goes
will always bring to mind
Ireland's Principal, Mister Jim Roos

Let's hear it for these heroes
They are family
They are legend
They are blood
Anyone who was here
for that joyful year of '63
will always and forever be
an Ireland Spud

Tiger Pa

You make your pro debut
age of two
national TV
chipping balls into baskets
with a miniature club
to make Sarge proud
Mike Dougla giggle
The audience cheer loud
A high you will chase
For the rest of your days
You bring a sport for the rich
To its knees
Like it's auditioning to be
Your bottom bitch
Like it's been freed of a demon
At your tent revival
Win the Open by fifteen at Pebble
Win it again in oh-eight
on a broken leg
Dominate the Masters down in Georgia
where you hole an impossible chip
Pausing the ball's logo
On the lip of the cup before it drops
Like it's a red carpet photo op
When a past Master makes
A watermelon joke
You send him packin'
To wherever crackers go
When they crumble
The days of Snead talking shit
about Charlie Sifford
and Lee Elder are done for
Your imagination so vivid
coaches cannot cliché
"Visualize your shot"
because you see and stroke
Extravagant works of art
when a simple fade will do
You adopt a different vision
You imagine the ball coming at you

It's the solution and the problem
Isn't that true?
Like birds flock to water
Balls and conquests fly your way
And who is a Cablinasian Ocean
To deny a single gull its stay?

I wonder if you foresaw
Your duck-hooking SUV
From the point of view of the concrete wall
Flying at you on a wounded arc
A betrayal of time and body would describe
It hasn't been the same after that, of course
Even oceans have their shores

I will always recall
A thousand heads turning in unison
Uttering involuntary Whoas!
when you smoke a drive
Will remember galleries clustering
Around a divot you make
With a five iron through
four inches of rough at Riviera
On a shot that swerves
around two trees
over a third
clears the front bunker
and stops on the green
Two hundred ten yards away
Like a tiptoeing burglar
Finding a hidden safe
They detective that divot
like it's a clue, proof
that the crime they witnessed
is the actual truth
I hope to see you to win again
This time playing one-handed
the last five holes because
A spider bit your hand when you
Fetched your ball from Thirteenth cup

This time wearing a saffron robe
after spending a year
In Tibet with Shaolin monks
Who are friends of your mom's
I will settle for a periodic spark
A memory of Mike Douglas's delight
When, after grinding to make a cut
you limp home on Sunday
and hole an occasional crazy shot
A rare sighting of the electricity
that once charged the game
like potable lightning
Maybe your children
having witnessed your demise
will shine bright because of it
Their light reflecting you
The good dad
Your young cats swinging
Freely
Ferociously
Seeing the future arc their way
Like a ball escaping the rough
Dodging trees
and traps
to land
pin high
at their feet

Eyes of the band boys widen

The Road Is Our Religion

Like a bird senses rain
I have known from the age of five
What is coming when
You and I take your pick-up truck
For a work-related ride

The road is our religion
This cab is your pulpit
I am your truest believer

"If a horse throws you off
Get right back on!"
You sermon through my not-good enough
My self-pitying tear-stained malaise
When a test is too much, a team not made

"This man we're going to see
He'll say words you've never heard—
Language you'd better not repeat, Son,"
You warn as we enter the barn of a farmer
Whose cussing could buckle a nun

"What the people need is outdoor recreation!"
You exhort of a fat little second-hand horse
Tethered to the truck bed in back—
That people will pay us to ride this horse
Is the holiest form of our faith

"You could hear the tanks rolling—
Then the shooting started—
Most were Americans shooting other Americans—"
You get that far and no more
In your patchwork gospel of what happened in the War

How great it was to witness the bug-eyed
Conversion of Creepy Frank, the local perv
Who got religion at the the point of the word
You delivered from here in a hell-fired homily
That put a sudden end to his nighttime
Peeping Tommery

Now here again, today, in the cab of this truck
On a country highway
I know what is coming
Like a deer smells a man in the woods

"Now that you've got your degree," you say
"Come back and partner with me
Outdoor recreation is the way
We can give the people what they want
Put us on the map. We can *this*... We can *that*..."

I scan the far horizon through the glass
Like that's where the words will be
I don't know what I'm looking for
But I know it isn't here

"No, Dad, no. I can't.
I'm leaving and not coming back."

Basement House Groove

Been around the world
Done a thing or two
Partied in Roppongi
Got lost in the Louvre
How it all got started
Where my trip began
Was groovin' in
the basement house
with Charles and Jan
Groovin'...
with Charles and Jan

Weather underground
Panthers in the street
Hippies out lookin'
for a place to meet
Took a bus north
Hitched a ride south
Ended up crashin'
in the basement house
with Charles and Jan...
Groovin'...
Underground.

All the long-haired players
from here to Kentucky
not a single one of them
could pluck it like Chucky
Danced in the kitchen to
The music of The Band
When we grooved
in the basement house
with Charles and Jan
It was groovy down there
with Charles and Jan

Coca-Cola might say
they taught the world to sing
We made our own music
Did our own thing
Got lucky in the lottery
Dodged the fuckin draft
Said to hell with The War
Socked it to The Man
When we were groovin'
in the basement house
with Charles and Jan.
Let's all groove
in the basement house
with Charles and Jan.

We're still groovin'
And dancing
And singing
And laughing
in the basement house
with Charles and Jan....

A Story About Maury

Maury and his family
were known to one and all
in the town of Windsor
which had one shopping mall

Maury had a store there
Trafficked inexpensive clothes
where folks of meager means
their wardrobes would compose

His racks were packed with bargains
Close-outs and remainders
Maury was like Santa Claus
with rescue dogs for reindeers

One day he got in trouble
for a most unlikely cause
Men from Maidenform complained
He peddled knock-off bras

When the other mall proprietors
heard Maury had been busted
They whispered, It makes sense to us
That Jew cannot be trusted

Who could make a living
selling cheapies like he does?
They reached a swift conclusion—
Maury must be dealing drugs

Like a Middle-Ages plague
the merchants' whispers spread
In Maury's store, the townsfolk hissed,
the tweakers score their meth

No petitions made the rounds
No evidence got got seized
Yet Maury lost his customers
like Fall trees drop their leaves

In October Maury heard the buzz
In November felt the sting
And for December's holidays
he did not sell a thing

In January just one shopper
came to Maury's store
A local meth head stumbled in
looking for a score

When February came around
Maury could not make ends meet
He closed his little store in March
and accepted his defeat

Serves him right, the locals huffed
that a Jew should take a loss
on a shop with no display
of Jesus on the cross

Seasons changed, as seasons do
When April turned to May
the town of Windsor's vengeful ways
blossomed into shame

Their daffodils exuded
The aroma of regret
Their roses drooped and blushed
In embarrassment

Hadn't Maury sponsored softball teams?
Done those funny radio ads?
Did he not emcee the talent show
and accordion the dance?

Was he not out in the rain
to bag sand in the flood?
Did he not roll up his sleeves
in the drives to donate blood?

Did a single soul apologize
or deliver their compassion?
You kidding me? That's not their way
They pretend it never happened

But Maury? He remembered
Did not wobble or back down
Opened a jewelry shop in a plaza
on the other side of town

Sells semi-precious gems to folks
and charges them to the hilt
for the baubles that they buy from him
to assuage their sense of guilt

What became of the begatters
of this tale's toxic start?
Their mall today is a warehouse
And Windsor
(thanks in part to a letter from Maury
to a college friend who's an executive there)
has itself a Wal-mart

Nineteen

I hope today you are breathing well
On a palm-shaded shore
Hope the path ahead
Holds twice the gold
Of where you've been
Hope you still dance the *joropo*
In purple shadows
On moonlit nights
Baby-moan at the sight
Of the setting sun
Scream at scary movies
Cry confronting beauty
Hope your brother still draws
Cartoons of you like he used to
That are maybe not so
Mean but just as fun
Hope you still sing Elton John
Spit blue in two languages
Have that laugh
Those opinions
The smiling eyes
Hope you gave up
The goddamn smokes
Don't take conspiracy
Theories so seriously
Or drink cherry wine
In such quantities
As we did—remember?
When I was sick with Nineteen
Mistook my fever for cool
Your kiss for a cure
My illusions for truth
And did not have the strength
Or the courage
Or the character
Or the decency
To say goodbye

No Prestige

We used to be inseparable
Birds of a feather who
flew with a wild flock
Two hands same clock
You were tick I was tock

Got into fun trouble
Or anyway the kind
we could get out of
before anybody got hurt
(that we knew of)
We were prayers
We were curses
You were vice
I was verses
Dom and sub
Water and tub
Sex and love

So what's the rub?
Where have you gone?
You don't return or respond
even when I drop a text
in CAPS and **bold**
Goodbyes are hard enough
Ghosting like you did is cold
Word is you're with a magician
Working as his assistant
Serving as his vassal
while he pulls old rabbits
out of second-hand hats
at Bar Mitzvahs
between bartending gigs
at the Magic Castle

Our love is a card
that's still in the deck
I don't care how it's stacked
Come back.
Come back.
Without you I'm a wreck.
Our story lacks an ending
Our pledge has no prestige
Our patent is still pending

I have always been suspicious
of the personal lives of magicians
The deceiving does not end, you know
when the audience leaves the room
when the lights have faded
and you're moving in the gloom

It's probably easier that way
when it's just him and you
Come back
Please come back
I won't ever dis-illusion you
Again
Like I did that time
Or two
My life isn't bound by deception
like it is
for a magician

Escape Room

Clue Number *One:*
You are a hostess in a Nashville bar
Who owns a bus you rent
To country music stars

Clue Number *Two:*
You get off after midnight and so do I
Multiple times
Best sex I've had in my life

Number *Three:*
I'm so lucky
You'll move in with me
To my place in Kentucky

Clue *Four:*
Nashville stars are
Slow to pay
You're cash poor

Five:
I give you a card
For moving expenses
You max it out by the time you arrive

Six:
You turn me on like no other
But when you come
You call me by the name of another

Number *Seven:*
Well this is an unfortunate twist
That Garth Brooks money is overdue
And you're going to have to sue

Clue *Eight:*
Is when your half of our
Rent and expenses is
Ninety days late

And here's *Nine:*
Money missing from my dresser
A twenty or a fifty
At a time

Then comes *Ten:*
My gun disappears
From where I keep it
Behind the headboard of our bed

Eleven is when:
I come home unannounced
And find you drinking with
A buddy from down South

Twelve is an accidental slip:
I catch your reflection in the sliding glass
Signaling your bud
To zip his lip

Thirteen:
Something I am just now seeing
Animals shy away from you
And I know I should, too

Fourteen's a beauty:
A cousin runs a trace for me
You've got three fake names on file
With Social Security

Fifteen:
Two of those names
Are wanted for fraud in Colorado and Arizona
Your virus is worse than the 'rona

Sixteen comes hard:
When you throw my stuff in the yard
I cannot call the police
Your name is on the fucking lease

Clues *Seventeen* through *Nineteen:*
Sonogram off the internet
Letterhead stolen from an OB's files
A claim you're pregnant with my child

Twenty:
At last the tumblers fall
You go as suddenly as you come
A day before the cops from Tucson call

And finally, *Twenty-One:*
After a month ensues
Tim from the Ford dealership
Rings me with the news
He's got those six Explorers you ordered
For the Garth Brooks concert
You told him you'd produce
I say to him, Dude, I feel your pain
Let's hope the damage is minimal
The woman is dangerous in twenty-one ways
And her turn-ons are all criminal

Hazer

You prepare in the bathroom
Of a rolling chartered bus
Carrying your college marching band
Back to its postcard campus

You've persuaded the seniors
With your intimidating charm
That a sophomore will be your mark
Though will not come to harm

Your minions pin him across a tabletop
Pants around his ankles, exposed,
His agonizing eyes shielded
By a *Playboy* centerfold

Every boy on the bus
Has turned in his seat to look
Upfront, the Driver glances in
His passenger mirror and—*what the fuck?*

Anticipation rises in you
Like incense at Midnight Mass
You are their priest most high
This is your What, they are your Why

They giggle as you emerge from the can
Wearing a bedsheet as your gown
A jockstrap for a surgical mask
A straight razor in your hand

Eyes of the band boys widen
Bus driver stares ahead at the road
As you lather the sophomore's wispy pubes
With shaving cream and an Afro comb

With a shaky razor you blade away
All evidence of his puberty
Down to his pink chicken skin
Streaked red where you cut into him

"Whoops," you faux apologize
To mirthless laughter from your acolytes
And silent winces from your victim
"Let me make it right."

You produce a tube of rubber cement
Apply a gob of its adhesive goo
To the tortured region of his loins
Where you removed his pubes

Ceremonially now
A baker icing his cake
You glue the clumped and
Lathered pubes back in place

In a seat across from your sacrificial altar
A freshman you'd selected to next
Receive the blessing of your blade
Cries at the sight like a bottle-less baby
And suddenly—
Like your joke fell flat
Your party got wrecked
You bat away the centerfold
From the hazed boy's face
So humiliated and sad
"Pull up your pants, you homo," you say
"Welcome to the band."

Later that night, the sophomore will
Bite on a towel to muffle his screams
As a doctor carves hardened cement
From bleeding skin with scalpel and benzene

While, alone in your dorm room, you
Conclude your interrupted ritual
With a masturbatory vision
Of the crying freshman shaving you

This is Not an Endorsement

We are entangled, you and I,
In all the hometown ways
Rooted in the same land,
Guided by the same hands,
Played on the same fields,
Ate the same meals,
Had the same friends,
Swam in the same waters,
Romanced the same daughters,
Prayed the same prayers,
Climbed the same stairs,
Laughed at the same jokes,
Inhaled the same smokes,
Took the same chances,
Danced the same dances
To the same songs
At the same shows.
We do have differences though.

This is not an endorsement.
It is an observation.

What I see in you is what I've loathed in me
My vanity. My needy parts. My holier than thou.
My "It was better then." and my "Gotta have it now."
My inability to empathize
Or see a different point of view
So much of what has haunted me
Is what I see in you

You knew how Harvard would play
Back in the wooded hills
Where we were raised,
The place I'd leave and to which you'd flee
Soon as you got the Ivy League degree.
And married the Homecoming Queen.
Looks from here like you hustled folks
From meth-addled places shadowed by
Klannish affiliations
Into a company Amos bought for you

That would pay you millions
And them pennies
While convincing them that a
Five thousand dollar deductible
Was the best you could do for their bennies.
And here you are, running to be Governor
So you can clear cut hickory and
Your sell your folksy French Lickery
To the citizenry. Me? I see trickery.

This is not an endorsement.
It is a realization.

You ship car parts made in China
On government-funded roads
To make the dough to bankroll
A campaign premised on fictions
That foreigners and feds are out to bilk us,
That invading hordes will kill us,
Getting voters to prefer hypocrisy to democracy
Is your fundamental skill, yes?
No doubt you're a decent man, locally speaking,
Driven to grow businesses, I get it
So why can I not escape the feeling
That people who vote for you will regret it?
That your true nature is predator
Stalking votes like rabbits in the
Tell Cities, Kokomos and Terre Hautes
With a transgendered single Black Muslim cat-owning-
and-eating lesbian immigrant newscaster on welfare Jezebel
as your one-fear-fits-all ghost?

This is not an endorsement.
It is an allegation.

I see how you cling to the coattails,
Of an artificially-colored money-laundering
Race-baitng, assassination-faking grifter
who clowns the differently-abled

Game recognizes game
No matter where it's played.
Over all this time and distance
You've come into easy focus
Making money and excuses
For questioning the validity of
elections and interracial marriages
and the ethnicity of a woman whose
skin is the same color as my granddaughter's
Shipping car parts manufactured
Overseas by underpaid Chinese
While building border walls to separate
Children from their families
And dreamers from their dreams

This is not an endorsement.
It is a condemnation.

Complicity

In case you are wondering about my complicity
In the annals and channels and backroads of Black History
V. Kali tells a story about her time in Ethiopia in 1973
When she is hanging out with Haile Selassie and Alice Coltrane
When she gets introduced to a pregnant cheetah and a couple of lions
The male's mane as wide as she can spread her arms
V., a lifelong friend of felines, gets along with the big cats
Sits with them, strokes their fur and scratches their heads
Like they are household pets with names and proper beds
Their keeper tears away a tuft of the compliant lion's mane
And hands it to V. to keep as a souvenir she has until this day
Gets on so well with the cats she introduces them to a friend
A deeply-melanated street-hard sister from Oakland
The big lion stands and steps to the woman with a stalking stride
As if she's a baby buffalo who has wandered from the herd
Whereupon, according to V., "That sister turned as white as Mike!"
That is the day, while a college sophomore back in Indiana,
Seven thousand five hundred miles from the Ethiopian savanna
I become part of Black History, even though it will be
Fifty-two years before I learn about it from V. Kali.

King of the Student Body

Sophomore

Bob from Fort Dodge
Drives an old station wagon
A decal in its back window
Says COLLEGE
Wears flip-flops in the snow
Hawaiian shirts to church
Long hair bleached gold
Has a ham radio in lieu of a phone
Carries a four-point-oh
Does not party
Makes his own fun
Says he's gonna run
For President of the Student Body
Announces his candidacy
From a fourth-floor
Dormitory commode
Designates the third stall
As his campaign headquarters
Walk in to take a piss
Dude's in the head
Campaigning for Prez

A thousand miles
From the nearest palm tree
He is a billboard
For sunshine

Platform

Robert Calhoun Kersten
Has us jocular and burstin'
At the pranks in his platform
The way he's ball-bustin'
Big city dicks from
Chicago and Boston
Who believe they run the show
Says if elected
He will abolish student government

Replace it with an oligarchy
Name himself The Prime Mover
Appoint a court consisting of
A Few Close Friends
Promises to award
Scholarships by lottery
Recruit students from
Rain forest tribes in Brazil
Turn the campus newspaper
Into a personal propaganda mill
Change the grading system
To only A's and B's
Conduct fact-finding missions
To girls' schools with
"Saint" in their names
Trains a stray campus cat
To sit on his shoulder
Names it Uncandidate
Makes it his running mate
Says if elected
The cat will be his
Vice President

Campaign

Our wannabe sovereign
Wears a Burger King crown
And a fancy vestment
He borrows from a girl
Whose uncle is a priest
His team is a band
Of small-town dweebs
Led by a short round
Hippie from Tell City
Who goes by the name of H-Man
The candidate gives speeches as a
Voice from a Burning Wastebasket
When seen on campus he rolls
With an entourage—

A dozen baller bros
In suits and fedoras
Carrying violin cases
Flank him on either side
A hunchbacked kid from Cleveland
Who goes by the name of Fish
Dresses like a Jester
And sweeps his path with a broom
He stages his own kidnapping
Holds Himself hostage
Demands a ransom
Of twenty-seven cents
Says twenty-seven cents is
The exact amount in his treasury
Says this proves his opponents did it
And cannot be trusted
No matter how they spin it

Vote

The people spoke
The government is a joke
The King wins in a landslide
Surrounded by acolytes
Our new leader takes to the mic
For a coronation speech
Says he spoke to God
Who told him to get the hell out
But Uncandidate the Cat
Urged him to stay in
Says he listened to the Cat
Because unlike Himself and God
The Cat is mortal
And deserves its earthly reward
Says he will henceforth
Be addressed
As His Movership

Reign

His Movership's reign
Consists of two Prime Moves
Move Number One is fun
He summons the Beach Boys
And his hero Brian Wilson
To play a concert at our school
Move Number Two is cool
The King abdicates
Names—not the Cat to take his place
But the short round
Hippie from Tell City
H-Man
Who would not have gotten
A dozen votes on his own
Becomes the greatest student leader
Our school has ever known
When he took off
His Burger King crown
Folded his throne
Found the Cat a home
Empowered a nerd
His Movership
True to his word
Became divine

A thousand miles
From the nearest palm tree
He is a billboard
For sunshine

*You have the eyes of
the ancients*

Rosie Is Here

You came with a storm
We'd had no rain for ninety days
Then BOOM!
Thunder!
Wind!
Lightning!
Rain!
God's boisterous orchestrations
Making one thing clear—
Rosie is here!

The doctors say you got here early
But we can tell you made your
Entrance right on cue
At a time chosen by you
Everything about you speaks of patience
You have the eyes of the ancients
Eyes that say we've met before
Eyes of a blues man singin' pretty
On a summer porch in Mississippi
Eyes of a nun in a mountain monastery
Who can solve a mystery
Without leaving her room
Eyes that open unlocked doors
That can cut through fog to find
A hidden treasure or a lost dog
I cannot be impatient any more
Now that I've gone for a swim
In that ocean gaze of yours

You're not the storm
You are the eye of it
Your encircled serenity
Here to remind us
That all storms pass

That what what we have
And hold close
Following thunder
Concurrent with lightning
Amidst the wind and the rain
Is you

Biographies of the Saints

Willie

In dewy morning footprint-tracking damp
Willie—black man in green khaki
Walks his mower from his van down a homemade ramp
Plies his trade as a grass-bejeweled serenade
Cutting the diamonds
Where young ballplayers later today will play
Length of limping gait, easy economy to his turns
You're not surprised one day to learn
The man is Hall of Fame at Dorsey
Tore it up in Albuquerque and
Woulda made the bigs but for that knee
That goddamned knee

Jesus

Later that morning, Jesus, the plumber
Assigned to your call by a lottery number
Arrives wearing khaki of a different shade
Beige, embroidered with his name
Enters your house like Olmos taking the stage
A mind as lithe as body contorts to fit the answers
To what you do and how you do it, his curiosity a dancer
Snaking neuroplastic pathways in his brain
Like he frees your kitchen sink and drain
While imagining waters no plumbing can contain

Theresa and Regina

In virgin blue, a sister crew of cleaners
Hired by Holy Name—Theresa and Regina
Dust off all the saints, polish Mary, Pine Sol Jesus
Scrub their prayers, mop their novenas
Windex hosannas to the stained glass saints
Their prayers are for the little ones
That they may never know the guns
Aimed by Sinaloan narcos looking for sons
On the run from lives of darkness
Or daughters to seduce with
Jimmy Choos and rides in fast cars

Mayo

Mayo takes over Tony's garage at the end of the street
Opens for business seven days a week
Soon cars are packed like slabs of meat on a picnic grill
The mechanicking changes from mañana to a-go-go
Mayo setting the pace, jumping from hood to hood
Customer to customer, like a competition yo-yo
He's come a long way from the shed in Tijuana
Where he got his start at the age of ten
Filing serial numbers off car parts for Papa and Tio
Ditched that shit and went legit a long time ago
But never forgot how, for his enterprise to thrive
He must move with the urgency of a man committing a crime

Ashley

Ash got caught in a web of love and lies
Spun by a man moving weight from San Diego to Van Nuys
Carried Baby Aria to term in a concrete ward in Chowchilla
Did a five year bid away from her girl
The hardest, most solitary time in the world
Today a tattoo on her forearm says Warrior
There's a woman in the system, Ash fights for her
And Aria, an age-eleven skeptic, knows well the difference
Between the those who fight and those who cause the war
Between a man's game and his intended score

Ron

Ron's brother did a long bid in San Quentin
For doing what the CIA intended
Got that cash-for-coke machine running in L.A.
So government spooks could fly guns to Nicaragua
From an underground warehouse at El Toro
It's all the reason Ronny Ballgame needs
To raise up a garden that's the opposite of prison
Where seeds are released by sunlight
From soiled penitentiaries
And real gangstas grow food for their sets

Prayer

I haven't been to Church in ages
Don't find clarity in stained glass,
My saints are in the streets
Baptized by perspiration
And leaks from kitchen sinks
Confirmed by calloused hands,
Gospelling with their work
Making sacraments of their industry
Offering food truck communions
Their own blood as sacramental wine
Moving with an ocean's patience
To lay the invisible foundations
For children to find their ways
In the belief that their stations
Will not be of crosses but of greatness
In the belief that there will be a day
And a time
And a place
Where the hymns of the L.A. Saints
Will be sung.

Maria of Bristol Farms

In a self-congratulatory fever
I wander into Bristol Farms
grocery store of choice
for the fourteen percent who believe
they are the one percent but are only
leveraged to look that way

Here they get their designer chocolate
and their corn salad with jicama
Not just any jicama
A man with plenty of time to spend
asks the deli counter lady
about the provenance
of the jicama in the corn salad
It is her job to know
To have a story about the jicama—
Non-GMO, organic, picked that morning
in a Guatemalan rain forest
by union jicama-pickers
wearing gloves made from
recycled party balloons

I am not here for jicama stories
I am here to splurge
To pay twenty percent more
for the look-goods in Bristol Farms
where Madonna shops or so I've heard
This chocolate will taste twenty percent better
than the chocolate from Ralph's
because it's Madonna's chocolate
melting in my mouth

I splurge without shame
That's how good a day it's been
Buy a ten dollar melon
A fifty-dollar bottle of whiskey
Heirloom tomatoes surgeoned from the vine
by the same scalpels they use at Cedars-Sinai
Spend two-fifty on goods that at Trader Joe's
would cost a buck seventy-five

I splurge on the charm of the
checkout woman here at Bristol Farms
Her name badge says Maria
Her frosted pink lipstick
shimmers on skin
the color of the Rio Grande
That eight-dollar Madonna chocolate bar
tastes better already because nobody
scans chocolate like Maria
Scans chocolate like she scans people
Reads barcodes in their eyes
She shunts a customer
to the next aisle over
Tracy, she says to a tense
white checkout chick
whose skin is a battleground
for all her concerns,
I've got a person with a full cart
(She means me)
Can you take the next person in line?

I already have someone in my line, snaps Tracy
Meaning one Chinese lady with three items
Oooh! It's a supermarket checkout chick *Fuck you!*

Maria looks at me while scanning
my fifty-dollar bottle of whiskey
Says, I could use a drink of this about now
The image of Maria and me sipping on whiskey—
Totally worth the price they charge
here at Bristol Farms

Tracy's voice whips me out of my reverie
like a cop tapping on my car window
while I'm smoking a doobie
Maria—what's the code for green beans?

Four ninety-two, says Maria
with a shake of her head in my direction
that says, This shit goes on

Tracy comes at Maria again
Cop interrogating my passenger
Maria—arugula.
Four ninety-nine, says Maria,
You can look it up on the list

It's not *on* the list, snaps Tracy

You can ask them to put it on the list, Maria says
Knows her rights
She doesn't have to tell this cop diddley
With the slightest nod at me
as she bags my whiskey,
a breeze passes between us
and I know what she means

What Maria means is that
she knows Tracy's provenance
like the deli counter lady knows her jicama
Knows a game designed to play a woman
with frosted pink lipstick
on skin the color of the Rio Grande

What she means is that
this would not stand
back in Las Cruces
White woman talking
to a smart Chicana
like she's the Help
like Maria's attention is
just another Cheeto in a bag
Tracy will empty in one sitting
and still be hungry

What she means is
I have your numbers
(as you know)
and you have none of mine

My numbers are numbers
that are not on any list
Numbers money cannot buy,
computer compute, squares root
or ICE identify
They are the numbers of Tamale men
singing, *'male, ta-male!*
at this instant in time.
The numbers of mothers smiling
at babies laughing in their baths
The numbers of songs sung for love
And conversations had by dancing
My numbers are the numbers
of *Tias* giving *quinciniera* nieces
loving but unheeded tips on fashion
The novenas I have said to get where I am
surpass any number of hopes
your sad ass has
You have *no* idea

What I believe Maria means is
You are clueless as to
the depths of my defiance
I work in the office
two days a week, you know that
Up where they appreciate a woman
who knows the numbers like
the back of her hand
Who appreciate frosted pink
on skin the color of the Rio Grande
I am a work of art, my Checkout Chica
as much as any green bean ever was

What I believe Maria means is that soon
Tracy won't have to ask for numbers
because Tracy won't have a job
here at Bristol Farms
Maria will see to that
Unless—

Tracy can dance
Or Tracy likes music
Or has a cat
Or goes to church
Has a niece or a nephew
Can cook
Likes to shop for shoes
If Tracy asks
Maria will be happy to share
any number of her many loves

This is what I believe Maria means
as she smiles at me and hands me my last bag
the one containing the whiskey
Says, See you later

I do see her later, one week to the day
back for that Madonna chocolate
It's really good, what can I say?
I choose Maria's checkout line
How is it? With you and Tracy?
In the next aisle over? I ask

Maria scans my eyes
for the barcode of my question
Smiles in remembrance
of its provenance
We talked, she says
We're good

What I believe Maria means
is that Tracy has a niece
And a cat
And they're good

Blewfoot

I feel his backbeat
Holding it down
A sonic tattoo
Marking every body
Right now
And now and now and now

Listen to his high hat shimmer
Like barbecue
Laid with hungry attention
By your granddad on his grill
Like this
And thisssss and thissssss
Ahh yesssssssss

Hear his snares chatter
Like a jackhammer played
By an artist in an orange vest
Drumming triplets on asphalt a
Chunk-at-a
Chunk-at-a
Chunk-at-a
Time

His brushes whisper
Like street sweepers rolling at first light
When they're the only sound
On the street
Shhhh-shhhh-shhhh
Shhhh-shhhh-shhhh

Here he comes up Avalon now
Like a mailman delivering
Envelopes of sound
Holding degrees from
Front Porch University

He baptizes the beat
Of belonging
To a place
A city
A church
A tribe
A day

On his kit
He is home
And the rest us
If we are not there yet
Are on our way

How You See
for Caryn

You are not a conspicuous consumer
I never hear a whisper or a rumor
That you've been binging or splurging
Your extravagance is with purging
You are frugal and abstemious
Cautious about where your money is
You shop for quality
Not frivolity

More's the anomaly then,
In your outrageous array of reading glasses
Cheapies you snag impulsively in sleeves
Of three for ten bucks each at Target
Decorative visual aids that come in
A variety of frames stamped with designer names
Or anyway the names of a relative
At Target you are paying not to know
If "Gucci" means Aldo
Or his Cousin Carlo.

These many rims lay about
In capricious ways and places
Like the remains of a knitting party
Like optometric pets in a literary zoo
Like you provided magnifiers
To students in a fly-tying class
Like an etymology posse
Set up a sting operation
With glasses as their bait
Hoping to catch a reader—

Here's a pair on a couch
On a toilet tank
Your nightstand
Top of the fridge
Kitchen counter
Coffee table

Two pairs in bed
Ready-to-hand
Like a couple of bugs
In a spider's web

What used to befuddle
Today brings me joy
All these glasses
In all these places
Orbiting around you
Like twilighting birds around a tree
Are light-emitting cracks in the case
Of the Nancy Drew-est Mystery
Clues to how your line of sight
Goes straight to beauty

All these glasses are passes
To a world unplagued by
Double-cross and mis-direct
A world where illumination falls
Friendly on every surface
Where patterns meet lenses
And elevate ordinariness into art
A world where clocks stop
So that time can dance
With Serendipity

These glasses you buy at Target
Three to a ten-dollar glove
Are glimpsers of your love
The world you see with them
Is one where I want to live

Cello
for Nailah

That low string on the cello
Goes straight to the bones
Past muscle, blood, sinew
Like Shaquille through security at ESPN
Like Buffy through vampires
Like Bruce Lee through Yakuza

I am sitting in the front row
Bones buzzing!

Recap

Been a year in isolation and despair
Time marked in slow dances and Door Dashes
Life under a blanket of gloom stitched with
Random threads of light so bright
They knife our sun-glassed eyes
And keep wannabe sleepers awake at night

Been a year of loss and mourning
Brothers and mothers and husbands departing
After a lifetime among us
We are choking on our alone-ness
The only tonic I have found for this
Is to make a poem

It doesn't have to rate a *Dayumm!*
Only spill itself onto a page
As fragments of a fractured brain
For depicting on the World Stage
The lens where negatives get exposed
And V. Kali says, "What we say *goes*."

So go we do, on Zoom you know
Weaving syllables into spondees
Matchmaking meter and rhyme
Getting jokey with a trochee
And tactile with a dactyl
We are what we iamb!

Bring here your memories
Of childhoods and broken hearts
Fortunate beginnings and false starts
Bring here your rebellious dreams
Of Edens where we taste the forbidden fruit
And while we're at it, we eat the serpent too

We inhale decay here
And exhale becoming
Claw at the sky
And imagine flying
Swallow night
And regurgitate the sun

Years from now
When a child asks me
How we got through it
I'll say we hitched our wagon
To a team of horses
And fed them poems every day
They knew the way home
And carried us back
To where we belonged

A Chitty Chitty Bang Bang Wedding Toast for Emily & Jeffrey

Many years ago, on a crazy errand that turned out just fine—
and what is marriage if not a crazy errand that we hope turns out just fine?—
I taught Emily, brick and mortar[1] of my friends Jerry and Becky,
and her sock and blister,[2] Hannah, a bit of Chitty Chitty Bang Bang[3]

On the occasion of this Otis Redding[4]...
when Jeffrey takes Emily's German band[5] to be his trouble and strife[6]
and they become more than just longtime jam tarts[7]
I would like to offer them a Holy Ghost[8] in the form of this lump of ice:[9]

Adam and Eve[10] in one another.
For every job that needs doing, may you have the April Fool[11] to get it done.
When it Andy Cains[12] and you find yourselves
in in an Elliott Ness[13] of Barney Rubble,[14]
wear a smile on your airs and graces[15]
and bird bath[16] through your bunny ears[17]
before you go to Bo Peep.[18]

May God bless your gates of Rome.[19]
Save your bees and honey.[20]
May your corn on the cobs[21] provide you with satisfying Captain Kirk,[22]
good cat and cages,[23] and lots of extra bangers and mash[24] in the tin tank.[25]

The Jenny Lee[26] to making your marriage a bag of sand[27] adventure?
Don't take Brad Pitt[28] from anyone who tells you how it should be done.
If some merchant banker[29] tells you how to do it,
tell them to cattle truck[30] right off.
Don't find whiskey malt[31] with one another
or worry whether your hot cross bun[32] is sugar candy[33] with a basketball.
It's all about the rubber glove.[34]
All about expressing the turtle dove[35] that's in your raspberry tarts.[36]
That's the Wilson Pickett[37] to many donkey ears[38]
of happy Dick Emerys[39] on the frog and toad[40] ahead.

Here's to everlasting rubber glove![41]
And now...it's Harry Lime[42] to Moriarity![43]

01. daughter 2. sister 3. rhyming slang 4. wedding 5. hand 6. wife 7. sweethearts 8. toast
09. advice 10. believe 11. tool 12. rains 13. mess 14. trouble 15. faces 16. laugh 17. tears
18. sleep 19. home 20. money 21. jobs 22. work 23. wages 24. cash 25. bank 26. key
27. grand 28. shit 29. wanker 30. fuck 31. fault 32. son 33. handy 34. love 35. love
36. hearts 37. ticket 38. years 39. memories 40. road 41. love 42. time 43. party

Jaha Tells You

Jaha captained a cheerleading team
Who danced and howled on behalf
Of future Hall of Famers—
Running backs romanced by
Alabama, Texas and USC
Super-hoopers who'll one day
Make millions in the NBA
You can be at a game
Where such stars are shining
Yet your attention will be drawn
Your eyes open widest
At what transpires on the sidelines
With the cheerleaders
When you whisper to
No one in particular
That squad is *the shit*
Years later, you meet Jaha
You will go, aha!
That explains *It*

She is still the instigator-in-chief
Whose truths bring the crowd to its feet
Looking for proof?
Let me tell you what happened last week

A young woman out from D.C.
Steps onto the World Stage
Illuminates the room with a
Light that has never known shade
She big-sisters a roomful of women
Like they just arrived today
Like they are here tonight to play
Until Jaha takes the stage
Says okay—
And in two minutes
Delivers a century of San Andreas temblors
Revealing geographies you won't find
On any formally recognized map
Flames arc from her pages that
Burn familiar histories to embers

Little Sis clings to her seat
Like it's a failing raft
In a flood-riled river
Whose banks are lined with crocodiles

Later, when she walks into
The night with her mother
The young woman's light is quieter
As she confronts the territory
Jaha has re-arranged
A bird deliberating
On the difference
Between flying
And knowing where to land

A Thing I Know

Where fresh-cut fields hold the scented memories of a thousand summer days
And a yellowing sun pauses atop the tree line to consecrate the coming night
Where the melancholy silence of the disappearing day gives way to creature songs
And random fleets of fluttering somethings dance to the dampening nocturne

I know I'm home

Where a kitchen radiates with the aromas of every good meal I've ever had
And an out-of-tune piano does not diminish the passion in a song
Where children play games that did not exist until a minute ago
And no one shushes their shouts or disparages their tears

I know I'm home

Where forgiveness is a junk-built bridge over a river roiling with alligators
And love is a blanket stashed but never tossed during a winter's desolation
Where we take a walk in the tranquil woods to escape the boisterous crowds
And kindness hovers over our time together like a child's storybook clouds

I know I'm home

When I breathe reminders that every breath is a blessing
Where I walk the soles of my feet gossip with the sod
When rooms grow quiet to hear a rider reminisce a horse he'd known
Though everyone already knows the story ends with the rider getting thrown

I know I'm home

Where the people have been, like ears of sweet corn, husked of judgment
And the places we visit have lost their strangeness but not their glow
And time moves to and fro like the wind shaking the big trees
that have been my friends for as long as I can remember
Just like you

I am home

Voice Mail to Bill Murray's 800 Number

Bill, it's Bonifer
Twenty or so years ago
With help from Joel
And hundreds of Serendips
I set out to find you
Because you had first dibs
On the title role in
The Legend of Cowboy Bob
A script I'd written about my dad

You and I met years before,
Drank Loewenbraus and
Yelled down at Melch from the roof
Of your place on the Upper West Side
You're the only person I've ever met
Who vibrated at my father's frequency

You know the improv saying
Never solve the problem of the scene
Like Didi and Gogo never found Godot
I never found you
It was a series of near misses
Like when I'd hear your voice
On the phone at Pin High
Where Joel and I were writing a script
And when you tried on Cowboy Bob's hat
After the member-guest at Pauma Valley
And it fit! It fit!

I was dreaming like Del and Viola
Of accessible intuition
Game is destiny
We go where it takes us
Know that your deliberate
Non-solving of the problem
Carried me to extraordinary outcomes
That probably turned out better
Than making the movie
With or without you
This call is to thank you for all of them

I chose to play the game
On a cross country sojourn
Because my life was in disarray
Divorce
Money down the drain
No end to the pain
I'd brought down
On people I love to this day
The game was intervention
direction, connection

The way the game worked
I asked everyone
Whose path crossed mine
If they'd seen you
A surprising number of them had
People really love you
You know that
Went places where your presence
Was as strong as incense in the Vatican
The statue of Jesus at Regis,
Wrigley of course
Meier's in Wilmette
And when the people I met
Had ideas where you'd be
I ignored them all
Never solve the problem of the scene

Woogie told me the story
About you and him tossing Ziskin in the lake
A day with Janelle in Boulder
Was guided meditation
I spent a night jamming with Jerry
In his Downer's Grove basement
And teaching Cockney rhyming slang
The next day to his two young daughters
One of whom got married
Yesterday in Tennessee where
I toasted them with the Chitty Chitty Bang Bang

Rene wrote a song in honor of my questing
Benjamin sang me a Navajo blessing
A girl starting her freshman year
Danced for me like Britney Spears
A giddy young lady at Wrigley
Said she likes sausages between her boobs
And flaunted Johnsonville figurines
At the intersection of her ellipses
Alberto, a young Jamaican filmmaker
Working at 30 Rock
Pitched you on his project
His homegirl Lise offered to cook
Quesadillas for us when we found you
I assume the offer is still good
And that there's a game out there
In the multiverse called
Find Lise with the Quesadilla
That's getting played right now
By players who will never
Solve the problem either
But will enjoy many margaritas on the way
Because that's how the game is played

I did a leg of the trip with Geo
To see our pal Pete in Greenwich
Who was on Lou Gehrig's slide
Who tapped in text-to-speech
Not lately
When we asked if he'd seen you
And when his machine voice asked
Who will wipe my ass?
We had a green light to tell
Shit jokes and shit stories
'Til we busted
"It was so big I gave it a name
And cracked a bottle of champagne
on it before I flushed it."

And quote movie scenes about shitting
"You fed a baby chili? Are you crazy?!"
Laughed so hard Pete couldn't breathe
Got out of phase with his ventilator
We nearly killed him with laughter
Which would've been a beautiful way
For him to meet his maker

I got it all on tape
All these people so enthusiastic
About playing the game
I took their joy as medicine
Their cooperation as tonic
Made a documentary called
Finding Bill Murray
About this ridiculous quest
That at last made perfect sense
When we showed it to Cowboy Bob
And a hundred family and friends
Projected on the side of our barn
At magic hour on the farm in Indiana
Ten days before he rode into the sunset
It was perfect

At the end
We chanted together
"It just doesn't matter!"
As our goodbye to him
And our thanks to you
For not solving the problem of the scene

You had that smile

Elegy For Uncle Joe

The fourth of her six children
got sent by his Mother
at the age of seven
to be raised by his Aunt Lizzie
her sister-in-law
who could not conceive
a child of her own

He hid all his hurt
in the azure of his eyes
Given a tin-roofed room
he heard the sound of his tears
falling from the sky
his pillow soaked in sadness
when it rained at night

He spent five years
wondering what was wrong
"Why me?" he would ask God
with his nightly prayers
"Why was I the one
taken from my family
and sent away from home?"

Thus forewarned
he did not believe his folks
when they promised him
after graduating high school
they'd pay his way through college
if he spent another year
working on the farm

The skeptical grad joined
the Air Force instead
Caught the bus to Fort Knox
even though his buddy
who was supposed to meet him
got feet so cold he froze
and never did show

"He lacks the fortitude,"
his Mother calculated
"The boy's too weak,
he doesn't have the spine."
She predicted he'd wash out
and be back on the farm
in a month or two's time

Well he showed her
and everyone in Indiana
he had what it took
to soar like a bird
Aunt Lizzie raised a winner
Spirit indestructible
An appetite to learn

Fledgling Airman Joe
was stationed in Biloxi
when he met Elizabeth
an Elvis-loving girl
who became his world
when he swept her away like a hurricane
from the Gulf of Mexico

So began their dance
The military ball
They waltzed around the globe
raising seven children
He reached the rank of Colonel
Eventually they settled
on Hayfield Road

He was stationed in Turkey
home base of the U2 plane
shot down by Russia in '60
We'd thank him for being there
to save the world from nuclear war
He would smile but never deny it
which is the way a hero would play it

The ever-ardent learner
got his Bachelor's and his Master's
in Electrical Engineering
from Oklahoma State
in a three year span
with four kids at home
Give Aunt Betty a Master's for that

He sent three young sons
back to Indiana
to spend two months
living on the farm
almost every Summer,
which must have surely been
his payback to his Mother

He bid the Force goodbye
after thirty-five years
He could've cashed out
like others of his rank
Been a Beltway Bandit
with a fat paycheck
and money in the bank

But he said "Naww,
I'm going back to school.
Gonna be a student.
Study jurisprudence
until I pass the bar."
He always did like
layin' down the law

Our Uncle Joe
would remove his belt
Snap it inches from the nose
of a misbehaving child
That kid would not
have any sins to confess
for at least another year

If you were on a pony
and he was nearby
he'd crack a buggy whip
to get that pony running
and learn you how to ride—
Better grab that mane
and hold on for dear life!

If your Acey and your Deucey
produced a big whoopsie
in a basement or a bar
he'd Billy Jack that game
shut it down hard
before someone lost their shirt
or the pink slip to their car

Our Uncle Joe
Aunt Betty's loving Beau
was Son, Brother, Cousin
Extraordinary Dad
Younger lawyers' Mentor
Pillar of the neighborhood
Pa both great and grand

When you were seven years old
you asked God why
you were sent away

In the course of your life
we witnessed God's response
The answer to your prayer

When Grandma let you go
she was gifting you to us
You were meant to see the world

When Aunt Lizzie took you in
it was so we all would know
wherever you were was home

We thank those women today
for the choices they made
for all of our sakes

And thank God for the boy
who had to ask, "Why?"
Now we all know the answer

For anyone of us
who ever prayed for love
you were the answer to the prayer

When we needed strength
that we didn't have ourselves
you answered with your own

Anyone of us who lacked
conviction or a spine
you stood on our behalf

When we could not find
forgiveness in our hearts
we knew we could find it in yours

If we ever questioned
how to be of service
you showed us the way

If we ever hit a losing streak
we didn't have far to look
You were our good luck

If we ever needed
a smile when we were down
you had that smile

Even when you wore a scowl
we could see it in your eyes
You had that smile

The smile that let us know
Your prayer was answered
And so was ours

Your life was the answer
You are still the Why
in all our lives

On this gathering today
as we say your name
as you grace our lives again
you are still our common ground
Our lasting inspiration
Our indestructible spirit
Our Dad, our Love, our Uncle Joe
Engineer who designed
The guidance system
That will always point us
where we are meant to be
and will now and forever…
carry us home

Last Night In The Buckaroo Bar & Grill

Jen moved in with Ken
On the same night they met
To him it was kismet
To her it was rent
Moved in like a burglar at a party
Who'd be back when no one was home
After snooping in his drawers
And jacking the password to his phone
She dressed to blend into his surroundings
Camo'd in country hippie don't-give-a-fuck
Fed his addictions to grandiose dreams:
Rockstar. Artist. Singing Cowboy
He was circle celebrating completion
She was his circle's bounce, its animation
He was captain of the ship
She was his star and wind
So here's the knot, the turn, the twist—
The higher he elevated her
The more she looked down on him

He bought her a violin.
She learned to play a song or two
Then traded it for a vial of blow
She railed in one afternoon

He got her a horse
She rode it in a show
Brought home an STD and an unlikely story
After which he rode alone

He acquired the house next door
Designed it to suit her television fancy
Including a studio where he kept his guitars
Called The Buckaroo Bar & Grill
She walked through once
And that was it.
Hated what he'd done for her
Wouldn't go next door again

He spied a black widow
Invisible excerpt for its red dot
On one of her black rubber boots
Later that day he wished he'd let that spider be.

When Jen's father passed
Ken played his guitar for the man
Accompanying his breath to the last
While she sat downstairs watching TV
The more he does for her
The worse it gets for him
Until one day she does him in

A hen with seven chicks
Struts over from a neighbor's place
To where Ken and Jen are working in the garden
She screams, *I thought you were going to do something about the fucking chickens!*
Slams down a shovel hard and sudden
Crushes three of the baby chicks
Mother hen squawks in spread-winged panic
As her other four chicks escape and scatter
For Ken
It is the end
Of them

That night
For the first time in twenty-five years
He does not take his meds.
In two days it is all he can do
To keep his head in the game
Long enough to put on his boots
And feed their animals

By the end of the week
He is eating weeds from their garden
Claiming they will cleanse him of the feeling

That his body and brain belong to a crushed baby chick
Believes they'll erase his sense
Of her looking down on him
From a horrible height
As he lays dying

Then finally—
Absolute clarity
He'd been an Eagle Scout long ago
And now he is again.
A Scout always has a plan
He waits until he's sure she's sleeping
Two ayem
Glides to the house next door
Into the Buckaroo Bar & Grill
Rope
Barstool
Beam overhead
Loops and ties with Scout conviction
Slack enough
Heads in
Lets go
Steps off
Light drains electrically
Into the sight of his favorite Stratocaster
And he is carried away in its wake
On a wave of satisfaction
Knowing now she will *have* to come
To the house next door
The house he built for her
And though the sight will be grim
At last she'll be looking up to him

Eddie's Carolina

I have attended all four schools of barbecue
Orally examined the ribs in Kansas City
Quizzed that brisket down in Texas
Tested smokey links in Tennessee
I got stained shirts like diplomas and
Eddie's Carolina here in this city
Is where I received my pulled pork PhD

Today Eddie himself has come out
On the patio to sit and chat
Vinegar-basted observations
And red-peppered opinions
Are specialities of his house

He tenders his loins with
"The things I do for my woman"
Grilled on a smoldering bed of
"These motherfuckers downtown"

His ribs radiate the aroma of
"Play the goddamn game like they used to"
Glazed in the brown sugar of
"Wouldja look at the ass on that!"

He flavors his slabs with recollections—
Steelers, Bulls, Elvis, Mavis—
Served with a side of
"Lemme tells ya what happened in Vegas"

What Eddie's dishing out today
Is a hog that found its calling
Slathered in "You see this shit on TV?
About the rioting up the street?"

He has only this week
Fired up his famous grill again
And got word to regulars like me
That we could come back and eat
"After the fake-ass quarantine"

Says he cannot afford for his kitchen
To be one more day out of commission

I give him my number
And promise my twelve-gauge
On ten minutes' notice
What I do not know
Is that Eddie has a
Twelve-gauge of his own
Sawed-off and outlawed
Hidden behind his freezer
Artifact of a time
When folks paid in cash
And he'd more than once
Been robbed of his bank
After locking up at night

Our shotgun promises
Do not anticipate or include
A SWAT team chasing looters
After midnight like one of them
Once hunted troublemakers in Al-Falluja
And never got over the high
Of merits the higher-ups awarded
For every neutralized target

Four of the seven cops
Have eaten here before
Recognize Eddie at the door
With his sawed-off
Six of the seven hold their fire
One blasts away at a memory
Of a make-believe Iraqi

On the tongue that curses his snafu
He can still taste the MREs that passed for food

Now where will we get our barbecue?

War Comes Home

By your distant silences we know
you are visiting a place where
none of us will ever go

By the way you flinch around
sudden sounds we know
you hear more than meets the ear

By your avoidance of boisterous rooms
we sense how you are seeking still
an exit from your wound

By your loathing of guns we can assume
you have witnessed the damage
such weapons can do

By your supper table references
to starving people we believe
you've stared hunger in the eye

All of which is why—

We must not take more than we can eat
and always eat what's on our plate

We reject armored weapons
as the answer to a question

We remove ourselves from the sway
of a surging human wave

We can smell a lit fuse
and feel a coming boom

We show respect to silence
as the residence of memory

You lift the curtain on the war
only a time or two

"You don't know where you are," you say
one day when I question you

"In the morning you hear the tanks
and then the shooting starts."

"Did anyone get killed?" I ask
trespassing on your reticence

With a far-off look you nod and say,
"Most were Americans shooting other Americans."

The curtain closes then
never to open again
though you planted a tree of truth
in a forest of unknowns:
We live and die with consequences
when wars follow soldiers home

Bad Goodbye

You'd always made it plain
You were the first to know
And what it was you knew
You could not say

Privileged intelligence
Was your stock in trade
It could only be acquired
For a fee

You fed your hungry clients
With the latest news
Educating them
Was your science

You gave up cigarettes
When it was too late
The one and only time
You failed a test

Every time we met for breakfast
You had "The Benedict"
That particular move
Was not your best

Was it smart of you to smoke
Four types of meat at once
Duck fat dripping down
On all the rest?

Now your days with us are few
Soon your light will join the stars
We have gathered 'round your bed
To see you through

We say a quiet litany
Of so-longs and see-you-soons
Un-mendable fray at the end
Of our path

I'll miss how you foresee
Things I didn't know existed
'Til you shared their descriptions
With dumbass me

I'll miss the lame charade
We used to laugh about
And all the brilliant moves
We never made

I whisper what I treasure
Of our days together
And offer one more thought
Before you go

Wherever it is you're going
May you greet it with
Your ever-seeking spirit
Your joy at knowing

"No, Mike! No!" you gasp
Turning away in your bed
As if I've pulled a knife
and made a threat

Oh wow, oh wow, my friend
Would that we could have
One more laugh right now
At my expense

This is why you never
Let me take our picture
Why you always played
Guitar alone

What I construed as your
Appetite for learning
Was actually your yearning
For control

Your curiosity
Was in reality
Your unrelenting fear
Of the unknown

May the looming shadow
On the door you're passing through
Turn out to be a friend
A gentle loving Yes
A welcome home

Last Words

Goodnight, my kitten.[1]
I must go in, for the fog is rising.[2]
A certain butterfly is already on the wing.[3]
Of course I know who you are. You're my girl. I love you.[4]
I love you very much, my dear Beaver.[5]
You are wonderful.[6]

I love you.[7]
I am wonderful.[8]
I feel great.[9]
Never felt better.[10]
Yolanda. Room one five eight.[11]

God bless. God damn.[12]
Someone help me![13]
Damn it! Don't you dare ask God to help me![14]
Excuse my dust.[15]
Fuck you.[16]
Toodle-oo.[17]

All my possessions for a moment of time.[18]
I'm going away tonight.[19]
I'm bored with it all.[20]
I'm bored.[21]
Take me home.[22]
It's me, it's Buddy...I'm cold.[23]
Just don't leave me alone.[24]

I'm losing it.[25]
I can't breathe![26]
You, too, my child?[27]
Anyway no one's in jail.[28]
I done told you my last request...a bullet-proof vest.[29]

Oh, you young people act like old men. You are no fun.[30]
A party! Let's have a party![31]
Are you guys ready? Let's roll.[32]
I'm going to the bathroom to read.[33]
Please leave the window open.[34]
The wallpaper and I are fighting a duel to the death. One of us has to go.[35]
Brothers! Brothers! Please, this is a house of peace.[36]
Thank God, I'm tired of being the funniest person in the room.[37]

This is no way to live.[38]
It's not so hard, Rock.[39]
There's nothing to worry about.[40]
Don't cry for me. I'm going to be with your father now.[41]
Wow![42]
Oh, wow! Oh, wow! Oh, wow![43]

Swing low, sweet chariot.[44]
Farewell, my friends, I go to glory.[45]
I'll see you at the movies.[46]
It's very beautiful over there.[47]

And now for a final word from our sponsor.[48]
Love one another.[49]

1. Ernest Hemingway 2. Emily Dickinson 3. Vladimir Nabokov 4. John Wayne 5. Jean Paul Sartre
6. Sir Arthur Conan Doyle 7. Jackie Robinson 8. Mary McLeod Bethune 9. 'Pistol' Pete Maravich
10. Douglas Fairbanks 11. Selena Quintanilla-Pérez 12. James Thurber 13. Sal Mineo
14. Joan Crawford 15. Dorothy Parker 16. Tupac Shakur 17. Allen Ginsberg 18. Queen Elizabeth I
19. James Brown 20. Winston Churchill 21. James Baldwin 22. Booker T. Washington
23. Truman Capote 24. John Belushi 25. Frank Sinatra 26. Eric Garner 27. Julius Caesar
28. My friend, Kent's, uncle 29. James W. Rogers 30. Josephine Baker 31. Margaret Sanger
32. Todd Beamer 33. Elvis Presley 34. Jim Varney 35. Oscar Wilde 36 Malcolm X 37. Del Close
38. Groucho Marx 39. George Gipp 40. My friend, Helene's, father 41. Jacqueline Kennedy Onassis
42. Bo Diddley 43. Steve Jobs 44. Harriet Tubman 45. Isadora Duncan 46. Roger Ebert
47. Thomas Edison 48. Charles Gussman 49. George Harrison

Nine Lives

One

Rage says don't let those fucks get away with that when you've got a Glock in the glove box

Two

Ego nudges her backward one more little step for a better selfie at the canyon rim

Three

Systems say do not hesitate to open fire on a startled resident at the wrong address

Four

Depression nooses a knot for the Eagle Scout just like his manual taught

Five

Confusion takes the wheel when he wakes up on the wrong side of the center line

Six

Exhaustion and his Meds agree it's okay to forget about that baby in the back seat

Seven

Fear answers her knock at two ayem without ever opening the door

Eight

Panic says make her stop when the old lady drops her groceries and fights for her money

Nine

Desperation encourages her into an arrangement with a calculating stranger

And that, says the Cat, is the end of that.

Shoes on Power Lines

Ha-ha, how cool! To hang
A pair of shoes across a power line
In Silver Lake after a night of song and drink.
Pry the Chucks off the feet of an alcohol-dazed
Kayden, Jayden or Aidan,
Knot the strings and let 'em fly
In repeated cops-be-damned drive-bys
Until, on the fifth try
From the passenger seat of the
Beemer with Texas plates
Driven by your date
They catch!

Such a sense of accomplishment
To chuck a pair of Chucks across a power line
Over Hyperion at two ayem!
The next day you return to point and laugh,
The shoe-loser too enjoying
The notoriety of his kicks
Testifying like testicles on a giraffe
To your animal house stunt—so rad!
You Instagram that shit
And copy mom and dad,
Comforting them with the knowledge
That whatever it is you're doing out in L.A.—
You're just like you were in college.

Then one day Gonzales shares with you
The meaning of shoes on power lines
In a different place and time.
It began, he says, with soldiers
Hanging combat boots
As a way of leaving wars behind
And returning to their roots,
Then came to be a symbol
Of gang-affiliated soldiers
Losing lives to wars in the street.
Here fell Rollin' 30s Blood, '60s Crip,
Harpy, Asian Boy, Fruit Town Brim.

And then today on Adams
At Redeemer Missionary Baptist
You see a funeral procession gathering,
Black hearse shrouded by
Mourners escorting a casket
A weeping mother near collapsing,
Hysterical girlfriend, hands grasping air
Blindly in her darkness for a
Light switch that isn't there.

They are here, you surmise, to bury Ervin,
Died in a drive-by four days ago
Four blocks away at two ayem
You heard the shots and then the sirens,
Now, here in his wake, a broken momma,
Lost lady, and a little boy
Who'll only know what happened
As handed-on family legend.

A brother holds Adidas, never worn,
White with three black stripes,
One for each bullet that tore
His kin apart at Western and Twenty-Ninth,
Laces knotted so they can be thrown
Like an Argentinian bolo.

The brother, ignoring traffic, walks
To the middle of Adams and lets them fly
Toward a single power line severing sky
Dividing a day you live and a day you die,
Misses, as the mourners watch in reverence,
Traffic stops in both directions
As drivers offer witness to
The ritual of a grieving retinue—
A page that must be turned
For a story to continue.

Bro slings his bolo skyward again,
Again fails to connect with the line.
And again. Almost. Not quite.
With each attempt the mourners
Hold their breath
Until Yes!—
The shoes hang over the street
Like teardrops on an angel's cheek
And this time with their
Exhales there are sighs
Of satisfaction from the mourners
Even an involuntary laugh or two
At the sight of shoes in everlasting flight,
Footwear as a prayer,
A lasting benediction,
Even momma finds a smile
That was hidden like a lost antique
In the basement of her grief.

Brother backs off the street
With his fist in the air
Traffic resumes,
Drivers honking their salutes
Recognize the turning of a page
So a story can continue.

As the assembled take their places
In the parade of cars that will follow
Ervin's body to its grave,
The little boy takes one last look
At the only image he'll retain
Of his father's dying
Shoes on a power line
That night, he'll dream of flying.

Remains of the Bells

What remains when the bells stop tolling?
Vibrations of the
Intentions in the
Reasons they rang

Echoes of
Songs sung in choir lofts
And piping organs

Shivers of
Souls left behind
Shaking tears from eyes
Memories of
When they rang
And why

I ring in the day
Ring it in!
Ring it in!

Bringing—
Prayers at dawn sentencing
Produce trucks to interstates
Children peeling out to play
Grooms and brides beginning lives
Toll the time!
Toll the time!

Until—
Vibrations still
Echoes fade
Memories dim
Tears abate

Then here alone I stand
Ringer of the bells
Once a bell boy

Now a bell man
Setting a day in
Motion is my job
What remains when the tolling ends?
These bell-rope callouses
On the palms of my hands

Versions of Us

One Point Oh
Collided. Coincided.
First in word
Then vision
Then body
Yours
And mine astride it

Two Point Oh
Game of hide and seek
Got lost. Got found.
Good hurt
Bad hurt
Who hurt more?
It wasn't me

Three Point Oh
Room with a view
Hypnotized
Tranquilized by purple skies
My vulgar eyes
Didn't see who was in the room.
You.

Four Point Oh
Silence becomes Sound
Sound
Becomes Word
Word
Becomes Story
Story
Becomes History
Becomes Future.
Becomes Now.

Five Point Oh
We can't go back again
History's locked behind us
Different doors will open now
And walking through them
Because we are home
We'll invite the world in.

Regret

The old man gazes at
The amber lens of a setting sun
Recounting his times for its camera
Visiting a War he'd life-sentenced
To a penitentiary of shell-shocked silence
His wild ride on horses he'd rescued
And pastured on his dreams
A courthouse reporter romance
That begat matrimony and six children
And the nightmare when six became five
How that almost did us in
Until he showed us how to dream again

Do you have any regrets? I ask

(Long)

(Pause)

Just one, he says
To the commemorating lens
I did not say the word Love
Often enough to my family and friends

(Hmm)

Seems Love has served time
In the silent pen too

Maybe its sentence was fair
A word like that can cut both ways
Belief and deceit edge the same blade
What's hard to do is easy to say
A badge after all is no guarantee of how
A person administers the law
Who the warden is at dinner is no indicator
Of the man he is behind his prison's walls

(I smile at the dwindling light)

(Who's he fooling?)

The old man jailbroke Love a long time ago
It's waiting for us now with Morgan Freeman
And a fishing boat down in Mexico
He invited Love to the party in a thousand disguises
Put it on the RSVP list under an alias
Checked it in under an assumed name
Placed it in the witness protection program
Living in our midst free from harm
Love has been here all along

Maybe the regret will be ours
For never telling him
We knew

V-72

For V. Kali in celebration of her 72nd solar revolution

She's no ordinary letter in the alphabet
Upper case or lower case
Cursive or print
Arial or Times New Roman
don't begin to convey
the meaning of this woman

Allow me to lay out
in pictographic terms
better than mere words
what V means to me
and to the people
in our community

She is the point where
isolated individuals
join together
and become one

The basis of an A-frame
A tipi, a shelter in a storm
Cabin in a forest
Home of shade and warmth

An arrow pointing the way
Piercer of armored pretension
Finder of tenderness
Deliverer of love

A beam of light
she brightens days
illuminates paths
spots who's deserving of a stage

Ramp for elevation
of those laid low
For those whose feet are failing them
an easier way to roll

Springboard to launch
notions to the sky
becoming arc and shape
of the graceful dive

Fulcrum to leverage
the weight of a day
into a poem that converts
believers in the dawn

Her blades scissor away
veils of confusion and deceit
to reveal honest answers
behind the doublespeak

Her algebraic formulas
diminish big britches
And create value-adds
to talent you didn't know you had

As our Illuminati
She sees through your ruses
poses and sorry excuses
like Bruce Lee chops karate

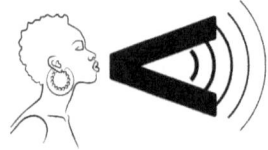
She megaphones voices
worthy of being shared
and amplifies whispers that
would not otherwise be heard

She is the old school antenna
that picks up signals on her
Magnavox Populi
that bring whole family 'round

She'll cone her soft swirls
in flavors Baskin and Robbins
and Hagen and Dazs'll
never dream are possible
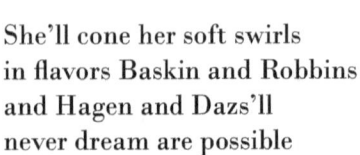

With her coaching we go for two
after every touchdown
She is our guarantee of victory
Our signaler of peace

She funnels colors and vibes
into a communal pool
where all who know her
share their common wealth

She's no ordinary letter in the alphabet
You won't find this V in a spelling bee
in your Campbell's soup
or the label of your juice

She is our beating heart
a work of living art
that we gather to salute
when she turns seventy-two!

Peripheral Vision

I spy the drifting concrete truck
In plenty of driving time
Driver drunk or asleep at the wheel
Drifting over the center line

Will I note the silhouette
Of an angry young man
Standing on the overpass
Weighing the brick in his hand?

I got an early bead on the Rottweiler
Straining against its leash
Insisting to its owner
I'm a threat to his well-being

Will I spot the stealthy Dobie
Lurking behind the trash cans
Extending its master's property
To the street on Monday evenings?

My front door and my back
Are dead-bolted and surveilled
I get notified remotely
Of strangers on the premises

Will I be able to sleep with the thought
That a gas leak under the house
Or a sparking electrical short
Is my concealed nemesis?

Even an occasional hiker like me
Can spot the uncoiled whip
Of a snake sunning itself
On the trail where I walk

Will I be alerted in time
To the reticulated viper
Resting in the half-light
Shadows of the fallen log?

Stacking sheets of corrugated steel
Onto the freight elevator
In a hundred-ten-degree heat
Ain't no fun, but I've got a job to do

Will I still be standing here
When one of the sheets slides
And shoots three stories down the shaft
With the force to cut me in two?

I meant to take a romantic tour
I'd seen and booked through a brochure
Had a plan for how I'd travel
Until a day it all unraveled
My path has not been shaped by dreams
But by the twists and serendipity
Of what I have caught and seen
At the edges of perception
Out the corner of my eye

Peripheral vision saved my life

Amen Asé Aho

Amen Amen Amen
I honor what you just said
Check a box next to the name
of a god we dare not cross
Bless the end of that fucked-up thing
we'll never do again
Our test finally behind us
we breathe relief that the devil
that's been chasing us won't find us
The court will suspend the fine
The plane will be on time
The prospect will get signed
Our battle will be won
Our team victorious
Our journey glorious
What we pray will come to pass
This visit will not be our last
And if it is…
this is our agreement not to grieve it

Asé Asé Asé
I support what you have to say
Pour libation on our brother's grave
Sign off on our deepest belief
Feel my truth in what you speak
Commit memory to this moment
Respect to your counsel
Action when our voices echo
I pledge allegiance to our muses
We're all out of bullshit excuses
We're going to make the play
Crown the achievement
Complete the quantum leap
May our names run together
forever in the credits 'til they bury us
And then some

Aho Aho Aho
Let's break this bread before you go
I believe in your creed
independent of its religion
Walk the circle with you
no matter what it circumscribes
Root for you no matter what your school
We bleed into a common pool, me and you
Bandage one another's wounds
with the cloth of concomitant purpose
and the healing salve of love
May the cloudless sky deliver rain
Make an oasis in this desert of pain
Comfort us on our arduous way
Let the end of this ordeal
begin the next chapter in our book
Let us move in six directions
Pick up what is broken
and make it whole
Reach the end of this road
we're on and keep on going

Amen! Asé! Aho!

Acknowledgements

In addition to V. Kali and the poets of the Anansi Writers workshop, my gratitude for guiding the creation of the poetry in this book goes to: The World Stage in Leimert Park and its director, Dwight Tribble, for providing the Anansi Workshop with a home; Hiram Sims and the poets of the Community Literature Initiative (especially L.A. Seasons 7 and 11—you are forever my poetry family!); Takira Briscoe, the Publishing Manager, and Emily Anne Evans, the Production Manager, for the Community Literature Initiative; The Sims Library of Poetry, its Manager, Karo Ska, and its ever-helpful team, which provides our community with space to create and perform, and our Music & Poetry Jam with a monthly home; Lonnie "Meganut" Marshall, Nate Jones and the Porch Jam Band who bring the funky music to the fine poetry at the Sims Library; Jaha Zainabu, who opens creative doors to which only she has the key; Charlene "HustleDiva" Green, who gave me invaluable guidance on this journey; the L.A. poetry community and its elders, in particular S. Pearl Sharp and River GahMatah Oshun, whose wisdom and guidance shed light on every move I make; and to Caryn Gilbert, whose love enriches my life in more ways than either of us will ever know.

About the Author

Mike Bonifer is a storyteller & poet, a founding producer of The Disney Channel, and one of the world's leading experts in quantum storytelling, the practice of co-creating stories. He has written or co-written six books, including The *Art of Tron* and *Gamechangers: Improvisation for Business in the Networked World*. *White Men My Age* is his first published book of poetry.

His poetry has previously been published in *Dimepiece: Ten Years of CLI Poetry*, and in the literary journal, *Rosebud*. He is the editor of *Shooting Stars At Sky: The Poetry of Play*, an anthology of sports-themed poetry to be published by Mama's Kitchen Press in 2024. Other recent writing includes *Me and the Mouse*, a personal memoir about his 25-year association with The Walt Disney Company and the 25 years leading up to it; *Betting the Farm*, a screenplay about his family's mis-adventures on a small farm in Indiana; and *Cryptosaurs*, a multimedia project about dinosaurs returning to Earth to save humans from extinction.

Bonifer has taught storytelling and improvisation for business at the University of Notre Dame, USC, NYU, UC-Irvine, New Mexico State University, Cal-State Fullerton and at several campuses in the Los Angeles Community College system.

He believes we live our most rewarding lives when *your* story and *my* story become *our* story and we inhabit worlds whose beauty neither of us could have imagined on our own.

www.ingramcontent.com/pod-product-compliance
Lightning Source LLC
Chambersburg PA
CBHW070143080526
44586CB00015B/1823